Dedicated to the legacies of

Mordecai Kaplan, z'l
Zalman Schachter-Shalomi, z'l
and
Everett Gendler, z'l,

Who each pushed Judaism
to become more universal.

יְהִי זִכְרוֹנָם בָּרוּךְ.

Blessed Are You, Wondrous Universe

A Siddur for Seekers
Non-theistic Jewish prayers

בָּרוּךְ אַתָּה, עוֹלָם נִפְלָא
סִידוּר לִמְחַפְּשֵׂי דֶרֶךְ

Compact Edition
with abridged and transliterated Hebrew

Herbert J. Levine

Ben Yehuda Press
Teaneck, New Jersey

A SIDDUR FOR SEEKERS ©2025 Herbert J. Levine. All rights reserved. No part of this book may be used or reproduced in any manner whatsoever without written permission except in the case of brief quotations embodied in critical articles and reviews.

Published by Ben Yehuda Press
122 Ayers Court #1B
Teaneck, NJ 07666
http://www.BenYehudaPress.com

To subscribe to our monthly book club and support independent Jewish publishing, visit https://www.patreon.com/BenYehudaPress

Ben Yehuda Press books may be purchased at a discount by synagogues, book clubs, and other institutions buying in bulk. For information, please email markets@BenYehudaPress.com

ISBN13 978-1-963475-63-0

25 26 27 / 10 9 8 7 6 5   20250610

Contents

Preface: "Living in a Prayer" by Dr. Shaul Magid	xi
Introduction	xv
Guide to the Transliteration	xx
Prayers for Specific Times of Day	1
Awakening to Gratitude	2
Morning Blessings	3
Evening Prayer	4
Prayer for the Night	5
Service for Morning or Evening	7
Passages of Song	8
Verses and Sayings for Contemplation and Song	14
Barchu: Invitation to Pray in Community	20
Sh'ma and its Blessings	21
Blessing for the Light and the Dark	21
Blessing for Love	22
Sh'ma: Affirming What We Believe	23
For Those Who Question	25
Blessing for Redemption	28
The Amidah (I)	29
Blessing for Ancestral Wisdom	30
Blessing for Strength in the Face of Death	31
Blessing for Holiness	32
Blessing for Change	33
Blessing for Kindness	34
Blessing for Justice	35
Blessing for Creatures: Birds	36
Blessing for Prayer	37

Blessing for Gratitude	38
Blessing for Peace	39
Blessing for Jerusalem	40
The Amidah (II)	41
Blessing for Ancestral Wisdom	41
Blessing for Strength	
in the Face of Death	42
Blessing for Holiness	43
Blessing for Change	44
Blessing for Kindness	45
Blessing for Justice	46
Blessing for Creatures: Manatees	47
Blessing for Prayer	48
Blessing for Gratitude	49
Blessing for Peace	50
Blessing for Jerusalem	51
Concluding the Service	52
Aleinu: It's on Us	52

Torah Service   53

Taking Out the Torah	54
Torah Blessings	55
Returning the Torah	56
This is the Torah	57

Entering Shabbat and the Holy Days   59

Verses for Festive Song	60
Blessings for Shabbat	63
Candle Lighting	63
Kiddush	64
Welcoming Shabbat	66
For Shabbat: An Added Soul	67
The Stars Come Out: Havdalah Suite	68

Candle Lighting for Rosh Hashanah	70
Kiddush for Rosh Hashanah	71
For Rosh haShanah: Tashlich Poem	73
Candle Lighting for Yom Kippur	74
For Yom Kippur: Self-Correction	76
Candle Lighting for Sukkot	78
Kiddush for Sukkot	79
Blessing in the Sukkah	81
Blessings on Taking the Four Species	81
A Sukkot Request	82
Candle Lighting for Shemini Atzeret–Simchat Torah	83
Kiddush for Shemini Atzeret–Simchat Torah	84
My Song for Simchat Torah	86
Blessings for Chanukah	87
Meditation before the Chanukah Candles	89
For Tu B'Shvat: Change Is Like That	90
For Purim: Dress Rehearsal	91
Candle Lighting for Passover	92
Kiddush for Passover	93
For Passover: A Hymn to Diasporah	95
Candle lighting for the Seventh Night of Passover	96
Kiddush for the Seventh Night of Passover	97
Songs from The Song of Songs	99
For Yom HaShoah and Yom HaZikaron: To Remember and to Blot Out	102
For Israel's Independence Day: All in the Family	103
Candle Lighting for Shavuot	106
Kiddush for Shavuot	107
For Shavuot: A New Old Religion	109
For Tisha b'Av: Birth Pangs	110

Blessings for Various Occasions — 111
  Blessings for Food and Drink — 112
    Blessings Before a Meal — 112
    Blessing for Drinking Water — 112
    Blessing over Wine or Grape Juice — 113
    Blessing over Fruits — 113
    Blessing over Vegetables — 113
  Blessing After a Meal — 114
  Blessings for Sight and Smell — 115
    Blessing on Seeing a Rainbow — 115
    Blessing on Seeing the Ocean — 115
    Blessing on Seeing Mountains — 116
    Blessing on Smelling Fragrant Flowers — 116
  Blessing for Reaching a Milestone — 117
  Blessing for a Transition — 118
  Wedding Blessings — 119
    Blessings of the Officiant — 119
    The Giving of Rings — 119
    The Seven Blessings of the Congregation — 120
  Blessing for Healing — 122
  Declaration on Hearing of a Death — 123

Walking the Mourner's Path — 125
  At the Graveside — 126
  Response to the Mourners: — 126
  For Those We Loved — 127
    For a Person who Died without Family — 128
    For Alienated Relationships — 128
  At a House of Mourning — 129
    Remembering a Good-Hearted Man — 129
    Remembering a Good-Hearted Woman — 130
  A New Kaddish — 131

Musical Notation: Thirteen Songs   132
   A Blessing for the Light and the Dark   133
   A Blessing for the Light and the Dark   134
   A Blessing for the Light and the Dark   136
   A Blessing for Love   138
   A Blessing for Love   139
   A Blessing for Love   140
   A Blessing for Redemption   141
   A Blessing for Holiness   142
   A Blessing for Gratitude   143
   A Blessing for Peace   144
   Welcoming Shabbat   145
   Welcoming Shabbat   147
   For Those We Loved   148

Afterword   149
   Acknowledgments   157
   About the Author   161

Preface:
"Living in a Prayer"

In the year 2000 singer songwriter Greg Brown released an album, *Covenant,* with a song entitled, "Living in a Prayer." It is a soulful song about seeking comfort and solace amidst chaos and confusion. It expresses hope without nostalgia, the longing of connection without romance, belief without faith. The song ends with the following lines:

> You should be here
> I should be there
> Long as I'm in your heart
> I'm living in a prayer.

Many of us are taught how to pray, some of us are taught how to *daven*, some of us even were taught what the siddur means. But how many of us are taught how to "live in a prayer"? The sages bequeathed us a siddur, a prayerbook that served as a map, both for themselves and for their progeny. Maps help you get from "here" to "there." But they cannot take you there, as Robert Hunter captures in the concluding lyrics of his song "Ripple": "If I knew the way, I would take you home." But the siddur cannot take you home; at best it can show you the way. The reason is that home is not a place but an aspiration. Home is not where you are, but who you are where you want to be. A siddur can teach you to pray, but it can't teach you how to "live in a prayer."

The Jewish tradition allocates times for prayer, a text from which to pray, and a structure of what constitutes prayer. What it doesn't teach us is how to "live in a prayer." In some way this is the project of *Blessed Are You, Wondrous Universe*. It does so by offering its reader a series of experiments in prayer, liberating prayer from the traditional siddur, enabling *prayer* to speak itself, as it were, into the world, through the human heart, up to the heavens and out to the universe. Its object is multitudinous; it is life itself; its subject is the human heart.

It is often not understood that in the more than 2000-year history of Jewish texts, the text that Jews through the ages were most familiar with was not the Torah, not the Talmud, not the Shulchan Aruch. It was the siddur. From sage to farmer, from merchant to peasant, Jews knew the siddur, they owned siddurim, often passing them down through generations. The siddur was not a Jewish text; it was a Jewish map. It was often a physical object to be venerated, a palace of Jewish creativity, often freed from the confines of the legalities and social norms of the day.

Reciting prayers often became writing prayers. The tradition of *piyyutim* (liturgical poems) flourished in the Middle Ages in Europe and the Arab world. Jews, and not only sages, and not only men, composed prayers of thanks for everything from local miracles to regional consolation, from natural disasters to human depravity. Prayers accompanied fasts for rain, thanks for harvests, for weddings, funerals, and births. While halakha confined Jewish behavior to certain norms, the siddur never constricted the creative activity of constructing prayer. This is the foundation of this present book, to free prayer from liturgy, to liberate the human heart from communal conformity, to offer suggestions of how to "live in a prayer."

Herbert Levine serves here as a navigator, a kind of Columbus of Jewish prayer, with a compass and series of maps spread across the table. He reconsiders prayer as a reaction to a series of actions in the daily lives we live: to react or to re-act, a gesture of response and repetition. Prayer as "re-action" enables one to step back from a moment in time and capture it through reflection and though language. Sometimes there are markers of Jewish life, sometimes simply moments in one's life in this world. Levine teaches us how to verbally re-act and live in a moment, sometimes tragic, sometimes celebratory, a breath of life. The prayer does not then dissipate into the ether of time, but becomes an edifice of commemoration. If you let them, these prayers may help you "live in the prayer" itself. And that is where wonder is found, not in the moment of surprise, but in the moment of repeating surprise.

Famously, Rabbi Nathan Sternhertz of Nemerov, the disciple of Rebbe Nahman of Breslov, wrote a book of *Likkutei Tefillot*. This was an audacious project that had never really been tried before. Nathan took each homily of his teacher in *Likkutei Moharan* and created a prayer from its message as he understood it. It was one of the great prayer projects of Jewish modernity, about which he opined eloquently. To fully understand something, he surmised, one had to become an active agent. There are numerous ways to do this, commentary being the most common in Judaism. Nathan had another idea. What if I distilled the "experience" of the homily by constructing a prayer to express its message? Maybe then I could understand it better. Maybe then I could "live in the homily" itself. *That* is Hasidism!

Blessed Are You, Wondrous Universe is an exercise in holy audacity. It suggests that living in the moment, acting in the moment, sometimes requires a re-reaction to instantiate that moment, so that it can be integrated into one's life. Not a marker but a key, not a memento but a code to unlock experience, not to pray, or daven. But to "live in a prayer."

It makes perfect sense that this new roadmap is dedicated to Mordecai Kaplan, Zalman Schachter-Shalomi, and Everett Gendler. Each in their own way tilled the soil for this project. Levine lives in their wake, and on their wave, and maybe even "in" their prayer-world. Kaplan gave it structure, Schachter-Shalomi gave it spirit, and Gendler gave it meaning in the here and now.

Don't re-cycle your siddur, you still need it to pray. But if you want to "live in a prayer," pick up a copy of *Blessed Are You, Wondrous Universe*... and enjoy the ride.

Shaul Magid
Cambridge, MA

Introduction

Welcome to *Blessed Are You, Wondrous Universe: A Siddur for Seekers*. This is a collection of contemplative and celebratory writing arranged according to the order of the Jewish prayer book, the Siddur, and the calendar of Jewish holidays. Most of the poems and liturgies in this siddur conclude with a blessing. These blessings are built upon the poetic convention that we can speak to the vast universe and to our Earth as a You, understanding all the while that we are part of what we address.

I wrote this siddur because I needed a Jewish book with which I could praise and bless in a way that would be true to my understanding and experience of the world. I also wrote it for all those who feel ambivalent about or alienated from the language of the Judaism that they inherited. Because I believe that there are profound limitations to both the current religious and secular approaches to Judaism, I have tried to create an alternative by forming a bridge between them. From secularism, this siddur takes its commitment to facts and scientific method. From religion, it adopts a stance of wonder and gratitude. Drawn from both worlds, it embraces a commitment to individual and collective responsibility for our lives. To use it, people with a religious world view may find themselves having to stretch toward seeing the universe and our world as a face of God that they can bless directly. Those with a secular world view may find themselves having to stretch toward the possibility that words like "blessed" and "holy" are compatible with the humanist premise that only humans can attribute such qualities to our experience. If the religious community reaches toward the secular and the secular toward the religious, then we might discover a dawning third way in Judaism.

I have found that most Jews who have a predominantly secular education seek access to what we can know of the world through our senses and reason. We have no need to hypothesize a Creator on the other side of the Big Bang, because we know that our human senses and reason cannot know anything about what came before. Though the beginning of the universe is still inaccessible to sense and reason, we can humbly acknowledge our awe in the face of a mystery we can never solve. Such humility moves us in the direction of wonder and worship. We might call the expressions of this siddur *secular spirituality* or *religious secularism*. I recognize that both of these terms are oxymorons in our culture, so detached are we from the feeling of amazement underlying both science and religious faith. I hope to recapture that wonder by finding a fitting language that allows us to nourish our hearts, minds and souls as we have not been able to do in solely religious or secular expressions:

> Let us praise the light that burst forth
> From that great and awesome blast,
> Giving birth to what lives and grows
> As sunshine nourishes the Earth.
>   (from "Blessing for the Light and the Dark")

Long before we heard Joni Mitchell's lyric, "We are stardust, we are golden," Einstein's theory of the universe taught us that we are made of the same elements as the stars. It is indeed time for this profound truth to enter our prayers:

> We are the love that shines through darkness,
> Our origins in the far-off stars,
> So grateful for our existence:
> Humbly, we honor the power that gave us life.

Where Darwin's version of evolution terrified religious folk in the nineteenth century — Tennyson summarized it as "Nature red in tooth and claw" — we who are secularly educated have long since integrated natural selection into our world view. I believe we can also integrate this concept into our experience of wonder and worship:

> We are the love that shines through darkness,
> Descended from those who came down from trees,
> Imbued with knowing right from wrong:
> So with justice, let's pursue what is right.
> (From "Blessing for Love")

The words of these prayer-poems affirm that the universe inspires our awe––what could be more awe-inspiring than the story of the universe! A second affirmation in this siddur is that our planetary home, Earth, is worthy of our devotion and protection. If we were to actively sanctify the cosmos and Earth, personifying them through the language of prayerful poetry, might we see ourselves as living in harmony with our surroundings, rather than dominating and attempting to control them? Might we become humbler about our place in the universe if we accepted our mortal limits instead of hypothesizing a future existence for our souls that makes us different from all other creatures?

There is a version of liberal Judaism manifesting in our time influenced by Kabbalah, the tradition of Jewish mysticism. In this Jewish alternative, God is seen not as a force or entity separate from the universe, but as the unfolding universe itself. Like prior interpretations of Judaism by rabbis and philosophers, this kabbalah-influenced Judaism tries to save the traditional language of the Bible and the Siddur, while using that language to mean something else by it. When liberal theologians and rabbis influenced by Kabbalah speak of God, they want us to mean the oneness that is all that there is. But why should we be asked to call the totality of existence God? Why should we call it by the Hebrew name Adonai, signifying lordship, when that word continues to convey to most Jews an all-knowing, all-powerful, creative consciousness that transcends the universe? In this book, I call the universe the universe, seeing it as a constantly evolving reality that has begotten us, the only creatures in this planet who are aware of the whole, of which we are but a tiny part.

Every day, the immensity and grandeur of our material world is revealed to us through images sent back by the Hubble and Webb telescopes. I believe we urgently need a poetic, soul-building idiom that conveys the wonder and awe we feel at what those photos show. That the process of cosmic evolution has enabled us humans to be alive to view them is just as marvelous and mysterious as the starry images themselves. "Blessed are you, wondrous universe!"

This shift from blessing God to blessing the universe involves a significant shift regarding prayer and personal agency. In a traditional siddur, God is the ultimate actor whose intervention we seek, whether through blessing, redeeming, healing, or forgiving us. In naturalistic prayer, however, with respect to natural processes, we praise the universe and the earth, and with respect to moral choices, we humans are the agents who need to hear our own self-reflective prayers. The prayer-poems in this naturalist book of blessings encourage us to develop a daily ethical focus on what we can make of the gifts that have emerged from within us. Its words challenge us to embody the central and hardest teaching of Torah: to love our neighbors as naturally as most of us love ourselves. We humans now know that we cannot exist without the other biological beings on our planet, who also need our love and care. So join in the swelling chorus singing the praises of our wondrous universe and our teeming Earth. Let's joyfully affirm our responsibility to love and protect all that lives.

Guide to the Transliteration

We have followed the system of transliteration of the Central Conference of American Rabbis (Reform) to assist non-Hebrew readers in participating as fully as possible.

Consonants:
　'ch' is pronounced as in the Scottish word "loch."
　'h' at the end of a word is silent.
　'tz' is a sound we use to get someone's attention; no English word uses it.

Vowels:
　'a' is always sounded as the 'a' in "father," and not as the 'a' in "bat."
　'ai' is the long 'i', as sounded in "aye," meaning yes.
　'e' is always short, as sounded in "ever."
　'ei' is the long 'a', as sounded in "neighbor."
　'i' is the long 'e,' as sounded in "cheese."
　'o' can be sounded as either the long 'o' of 'oh' or the slightly shorter 'o' of "boss."
　'u' is always long, as sounded in "moo."

Marks:
　An apostrophe between two letters signifies that the two sounds are to be elided, with minimal vocalization between them. Dashes indicate a new syllable in the same word.

A Siddur for Seekers

Prayers for Specific Times of Day

Awakening to Gratitude

I thank you, living and enduring universe,
That I am aware of my breath.
How great are your wonders!

אוֹדֶה לְךָ עוֹלָם חַי וְקַיָּם,
שֶׁאֲנִי עֵר לְנִשִׁימָתִי.
מַה נִפְלָאִים מַעֲשֶׂיךָ!

Odeh l'cha olam chai v'kayam
she-ani eir lin'shimati.
mah nifla-im maasecha!

Morning Blessings

Wondrous universe, my body works:
What must be closed stays closed.
What must be open stays open.
Awesome cosmos, my breath circulates:
What I breathe out, the trees breathe in,
What the trees breathe out, I breathe in.
Infinite universe, I ask myself:
If I am not for myself, who will be for me?
And if I am only for myself, what am I?
And, if not now, when?
Blessed living planet, you give me strength.
Blessed providing world, you satisfy my needs.
Blessed are you, wondrous universe, each day!

בְּרוּכָה אַתְּ, תֵּבֵל חַיָּה,
שֶׁנּוֹתֶנֶת לִי כּוֹחַ.
בְּרוּכָה אַתְּ, תֵּבֵל מְסַפֶּקֶת,
שֶׁמַּשְׂבִּיעָה אֶת כָּל צְרָכַי.
בָּרוּךְ אַתָּה, עוֹלָם נִפְלָא, יוֹם יוֹם!

Bruchah at, teiveil chayah,
shenotenet li ko-ach.
Bruchah at, teiveil mesapeket,
shemasbi-a et kol tzrachai.
Baruch ata, olam nifla, yom yom!

Evening Prayer

Have I acted honorably today?
Have I blessed others?
Comforted them?
Delighted in something?
Expressed myself clearly?
Fulfilled my promises?
Given generously to those in need?
Hugged?
Inspired?
Judged others for the good?
Learned?
Managed my temper?
Navigated between obstacles?
Opened myself to others?
Persevered?
Questioned unjust authority?
Repaired?
Spoken positively?
Tried my best?
Understood others?
Valued others?
Waited patiently?
Yearned for the good?
Tomorrow, may I do still better!

Prayer for the Night

On this night, may our homes be secure
And may we sleep in peace until morning.
May we think of all those who do not sleep
Securely tonight,
And may we toil for the night when all
Will lie down in peace.

בַּלַּיְלָה הַזֶּה
יִהְיוּ בָּתֵּינוּ שְׁלֵוִים
וְנִישַׁן בְּשָׁלוֹם עַד בּוֹקֶר.
נַחֲשׁוֹב עַל כָּל אֵלֶה שֶׁיְּשֵׁנִים
לְלֹא שַׁלְוָה בַּלַּיְלָה הַזֶּה
וּנְיַגֵּעַ לְלַיְלָה
שֶׁבּוֹ יִשְׁנוּ כּוּלָם בְּשָׁלוֹם.

Balailah hazeh
yih'yu vateinu shleivim
v'nishan b'shalom ad boker.
Nachshov al kol eileh she-y'sheinim
l'lo shalvah balailah hazeh
un'yagei-a l'lailah
shebo yishnu chulam b'shalom.

Service for Morning or Evening

Passages of Song

Awake to our wondrous universe,
We sing our praise and gratitude.

עֵרִים בְּקֶרֶב יְקוּמֵנוּ הַנִפְלָא,
אֲנַחְנוּ שָׁרִים שֶׁבַח וְהוֹדָיָה.

*Eirim b'kerev y'kumeinu hanifla,
anachnu sharim shevach v'hodayah.*

1.

If you call the earth your mother
Who gave birth to you in pain
From the wombs of all the mothers
From Eve until now,
If you call the world
Your friend who upholds you,
Whether in a day of trouble or of joy,
If you call the universe your helpmeet,
Who gives strength to both
Your weakness and your might,
Then join with me and let's sing in a world
That fills our springs with blessings.

אִם תִּקְרְאִי לָאֲדָמָה אִמָּה,
שֶׁהוֹלִידָה אוֹתָךְ בְּעֶצֶב
מֵרַחֲמֵי הָאִמּוֹת מֵחַוָּה עַד עַכְשָׁיו,
אִם תִּקְרָא לְעוֹלָם חָבֵר שֶׁתּוֹמֵךְ בָּךְ
בְּיוֹם צָרָה אוֹ בְיוֹם שִׂמְחָה,

אִם תִּקְרָאִי לַיְקוּם עֵזֶר כְּנֶגְדֵּךְ
הַנּוֹתֵן כּוֹחַ לְחוּלְשָׁתֵךְ וְגַם לְעָצְמָתֵךְ,
תִּצְטָרֵף אֵלַי וְנָשִׁירָה יַחַד בְּעוֹלָם
שֶׁמְּמַלֵּא מַעְיָנוֹתֵינוּ בִּבְרָכוֹת.

Im tikra-i laadamah imah,
sheholidah otach b'etzev
meirachamei haimot
meiChava ad achshav,
im tikra la-olam chaver
shetomeich b'cha
b'yom tzara o v'yom simchah,
im tikra-i lay'kum eizer k'negdeich
hanotein ko-ach l'chulshateich
v'gam l'otzmateich,
titztaref eilai v'nashira yachad
b'olam she-m'malei
mayanoteinu bivrachot.

2.

We praise you, vast universe,
For you inspire awe.
We praise you, bright and dim stars,
For you show us the distant past.
We praise you, shining sun,
For you give light and life.
We praise you, fertile earth,
For your fruits overflow.
We praise you, living beings,
For you are all marvelous.

3.

Planet orbiting the sun
From time's beginning until its end,
Planet, blue, green, and white,
Planet, covered with water and land and sky,
Planet made of forests, lakes, and seas,
Fields, and sandy beaches,
Planet Earth that we have seen from space
Complete and alive
Before our astonished eyes!

4.

They say that life began
Through a crack in the ocean floor,
That heat rose and still rises
From the core of the earth,
Catalyzing the salty waters,
Giving birth to life-forming acids,
In them the genealogy of life
In the sea, on land and in the air.
The psalmist sings,
"With you is the Source of life."
Every day, I too acknowledge
The source of life
That still enlivens my breath.

5.

From students of the cosmos,
I've learned that the elements in me
Were forged in the same furnace
As the stars.
From other great ones, I learn to sit,
Breathe, pay attention,
With eyes open to a world
Filled with glory and wonders
Like me, like you,
And like the stars.

6.

All my life
I've been blessing the grandmother
Who taught me to say
'Good Morning' to the trees
And the clouds and the sun,
Which bless me every day.

7.

I haven't yet blessed my childhood bully
Who had twenty pounds on me
And often hit me.
If I saw him today,
I would hug him.

8.

I bless again the goodness of my neighbor
Who brought me chicken soup when I was sick,
The neighbor who drove me to the airport
After I'd spent most of my money on the trip,
And the stranger who said hello to me on the bus,
Even though she'd never seen me before.

9.

In my childhood, I learned to bless God
To be grateful for my life.
Today I bless the world
For gifts arriving without a sender.
In my childhood, I learned to bless forever.
Today, with no certain future,
I bless everything
That will surely vanish.

10.

Attend:
This
Moment,
This
Breath:
No
Other.

Blessed are you, living world,
Singing a new song each day.

בְּרוּכָה אַתְּ, תֵּבֵל חַיָּה,
שֶׁשָּׁרָה שִׁירָה חֲדָשָׁה בְּכָל יוֹם.

*Bruchah at, teiveil chayah,
shesharah shirah chadashah
b'chol yom.*

Verses and Sayings for Contemplation and Song

1.

Who desires long life and goodness?
Keep your tongue from evil
And your lips from speaking falsehood.
Stay away from wickedness and do what's right,
Seek and pursue peace.

מִי הָאִישׁ הֶחָפֵץ חַיִּים, אֹהֵב יָמִים לִרְאוֹת טוֹב:
נְצוֹר לְשׁוֹנְךָ מֵרָע וּשְׂפָתֶיךָ מִדַּבֵּר מִרְמָה.
סוּר מֵרָע וַעֲשֵׂה טוֹב, בַּקֵּשׁ שָׁלוֹם וְרָדְפֵהוּ.

*Mi ha-ish hechafeitz cha-yim,
oheiv yomim lir'ot tov:
n'tzor l'shoncha meira
us'fatecha midabeir mirmah.
Sur meira v'asei tov,
bakesh shalom v'rodfeihu.*
(Psalm 34: 14-15)

2.

Let us learn to number our days
So we can get wise hearts.

לִמְנוֹת יָמֵינוּ כֵּן הוֹדַע וְנָבִא לְבַב חָכְמָה.

Limnot yomeinu kein hoda
v'navi l'vav chochmah.
(Psalm 90: 12)

3.

I have taught myself to be content,
Like a weaned child and its mother,
like a weaned child in my mind.

שִׁוִּיתִי וְדוֹמַמְתִּי נַפְשִׁי
כְּגָמוּל עֲלֵי אִמּוֹ,
כַּגָּמֻל עָלַי נַפְשִׁי.

Shiviti v'domamti nafshi
k'gamul alei imo,
k'gamul alei nafshi.
(Psalm 131: 1-2, excerpted)

4.

How good and pleasant it is
When all dwell together as one.

הִנֵּה מַה טּוֹב וּמַה נָּעִים
שֶׁבֶת כּוּלָם גַּם יַחַד.

Hinei mah tov umah na-im
shevet kulam gam yachad.
(Psalm 133: 1, adapted)

5.

Nations shall not lift their swords
Against one another,
Nor shall they learn war anymore.

לֹא יִשָּׂא גוֹי אֶל גוֹי חֶרֶב,
לֹא יִלְמְדוּ עוֹד מִלְחָמָה.

*Lo yisa goy el goy cherev
Lo yilm'du od milchamah.*
(Isaiah 2:4)

6.

May a new light shine over Zion;
May we all speedily merit its radiance.

אוֹר חָדָשׁ עַל צִיּוֹן תָּאִיר
וְנִזְכֶּה כֻלָּנוּ מְהֵרָה לְאוֹרוֹ.

*Or chadash al Tzion ta-ir
v'nizkeh chulanu
m'heira l'oro.*
(Siddur)

7.

The world stands on three things:
On Torah,

On service
And on deeds of kindness.

עַל שְׁלוֹשָׁה דְבָרִים הָעוֹלָם עוֹמֵד:
עַל הַתּוֹרָה
וְעַל הָעֲבוֹדָה
וְעַל גְּמִילוּת חֲסָדִים.

*Al shloshah d'varim
ha-olam omeid:
al hatorah,
v'al haavodah
v'al g'milut chasadim.*
(Ethics of the Sages, 1:2)

8.

It is not on you to complete the work,
But you are not free to desist from it.

לֹא עָלֶיךָ הַמְּלָאכָה לִגְמוֹר,
וְלֹא אַתָּה בֶן חוֹרִין לִבָּטֵל מִמֶּנָּה.

*Lo alecha hamlachah ligmor,
v'lo ata ben chorin
libateil mimenah.*
(Ethics of the Sages, 2:16)

9.

Do not look at the outside,
But at what's inside.

אַל תִּסְתַּכֵּל בַּקַּנְקַן אֶלָּא בְּמַה שֶּׁיֵּשׁ בּוֹ.

*Al tistakeil bakankan
ela b'mah sheyesh bo.*
(Ethics of the Sages, 4:20)

10.

Rabbi Akiva said:
"Love your neighbor as yourself.
This is the great principle of Torah."

אָמַר רַבִּי עֲקִיבָה:
'וְאָהַבְתָּ לְרֵעֲךָ כָּמוֹךָ:
זֶה כְּלָל גָּדוֹל בַּתּוֹרָה'.

*Amar rabi Akiva:
v'ahavta l'rei-acha kamocha:
zeh k'lal gadol baTorah*
(B'reishit Rabbah, 24:7)

11.

All the world is just a narrow bridge.
Above all, do not make yourself afraid.

כֹּל הָעוֹלָם כּוּלוֹ גֶּשֶׁר צַר מְאֹד
וְהָעִיקָר לֹא לְהִתְפַּחֵד כְּלָל.

Kol ha-olam kulo
gesher tzar m'od
v'ha-ikar
lo l'hitpacheid k'lal.

(R. Nachman of Breslov, *Likutei Moharan* II, 48)

Barchu: Invitation to Pray in Community

Leader:
Join me to praise
The awesome universe we live in.

בָּרְכוּ אֶת הָעוֹלָם הֶעָצוּם.

Barchu et ha-olam he-atzum.

Community:
Let us praise our world
And recognize what's good in it.

נְבָרֵךְ אֶת עוֹלָמֵנוּ וְנַכִּיר בְּטוּבוֹ.

N'vareich et olameinu
v'nakir b'tuvo.

Together:
May we grow the good of our world
For generations to come.

נִזְכֶּה לְהַעֲצִים אֶת טוּבוֹ לְדוֹרֵי דוֹרוֹת.

Nizkeh l'haatsim et tuvo
l'dorei dorot.

Sh'ma and its Blessings

Blessing for the Light and the Dark

Let us praise the light that burst forth
From that great and awesome blast
Giving birth to what lives and grows
As sunshine nourishes the Earth.
In the voids of the cosmos
Through time and space,
The glorious first light still shines.

Let us praise the soothing darkness
That ends the tasks of each day,
A cradle song for our souls
Longing for fresh mornings.
In the voids of the cosmos
Through time and space,
Awesome darkness encompasses all.

Blessed are you, infinite universe,
Revealing the light and the dark.

בָּרוּךְ אַתָּה, יְקוּם אֵינְסוֹפִי,
גּוֹלֵל אוֹר מִפְּנֵי חוֹשֶׁךְ וְחוֹשֶׁךְ מִפְּנֵי אוֹר.

Baruch ata, y'kum einsofi,
golel or mipnei choshech
v'choshech mipnei or.

Blessing for Love

We are the love that shines through darkness,
Our origins in the far-off stars,
So grateful for our existence:
Humbly, we honor the power that gave us life.

We are the love that shines through darkness,
Descended from those who came down from trees,
Imbued with knowing right from wrong:
So with justice, let's pursue what is right.

We are the love that shines through darkness,
A radiance so bright it lights up the world,
Carrying the love of generations:
With strength, let's chant songs of love.

Blessed are you, O shining world,
Reveling in love.

בְּרוּכָה אַתְּ, תֵּבֵל זוֹהֶרֶת,
הַמִתְעַנֶּגֶת בְּאַהֲבָה.

Bruchah at teiveil zoheret,
hamitaneget b'ahavah.

Sh'ma: Affirming What We Believe

Listen, O Jewish People,
Our world is our home,
Our world is one.

שְׁמַע יִשְׂרָאֵל:
עוֹלָמֵנוּ בֵּיתֵנוּ,
עוֹלָמֵנוּ אֶחָד.

*Sh'ma Yisrael:
olameinu beiteinu,
olameinu echad.*

Let us protect our Earth
For everything that lives and grows;
Let's love its beauty and praise its complexity.
Blessed is the place where we live—
For us there is no other.
We bless you, planetary home,
And all who dwell thereon.
We praise you, awesome cosmos,
And all that is in you!

May these words
Which we speak today
Be in our hearts.
May we repeat them
to our sons and daughters.
May they repeat them
To their daughters and sons,
For as long as they have breath to sing.

יִהְיוּ הַדְּבָרִים הָאֵלֶה
אֲשֶׁר אֲנַחְנוּ אוֹמְרִים הַיוֹם
עַל לְבָבֵנוּ,
וּנְשַׁנֵּן אוֹתָם
לְבָנֵינוּ וְלִבְנוֹתֵינוּ
וְהֵם יְשַׁנְּנוּ אוֹתָם
לִבְנוֹתֵיהֶם וְלִבְנֵיהֶם אַחֲרֵיהֶם,
כָּל עוֹד שְׁרוּחָם
מְעוֹרֵר אוֹתָם לָשִׁיר.

Yih'yu ha-d'varim ha-eileh
asher anachnu omrim hayom
al l'vaveinu,
un'shanen otam
l'vaneinu v'livnoteinu
v'hem yishan'nu otam
liv'noteihem v'livneihem achareihem,
kol od sherucham
m'oreir otam lashir.

After the Sh'ma:

For Those Who Question

1.

There are many worlds in our world.
For every man or woman, for every boy or girl,
A unique world:
Living in another's world takes immense effort.

2.

Believers say there is a world that is seen
And a world that is unseen.
As for me, what I don't see, I feel
Here on earth, between me and you and you.

3.

The wise ones of Greece thought
That we are two, body and soul.
Without a body,
How can the soul aspire?
And without soulfulness,
Everything is the body desiring
Until it bursts.

4.

Mystics of every religion say
That the world is nothing:
Zero and one equal zero—not one—
And so on
Through the rest of the numbers and stories.
Searchers of the sky say
That ninety-five percent of all that is
Is dark, truly nothing:
Who am I to quibble over five percent?

5.

There are those who say that everything is God
And there are those who say
That everything shows there is no God:
In a curved universe,
Opposite forces touch.

6.

If I entirely open my soul to another,
I disappear.
If I close my soul to another,
He or she disappears.
Our realities are dependent
On our keeping our souls
Half-open and half-closed,
Like the membranes of cells.

7.

For our song, there is no end.
May all times be favorable
For those who return with questions
About one
And two
And nothing.

Blessing for Redemption

I believe with perfect faith
We came out of Egypt to testify
There are narrow straits in every place
That all people must pass through
To march toward a promised land
That we will not reach,
But won't ever disappear from our eyes.

Blessed are you, singular planet,
Whispering redemption.

בְּרוּכָה אַתְּ, תֵּבֵל יְחִידָה
הַלוֹחֶשֶׁת גְּאוּלָה.

*Bruchah at, teiveil y'chidah,
halocheshet g'ulah.*

The Amidah (I)

Jewish prayer services offer the opportunity to align ourselves with our tradition's deepest values as we pause, reflect, and take stock of our lives. In rabbinic sources, the phrases "the prayer" or "the standing prayer" (Amidah) refer to the multi-part daily prayer composed of petitions that end with blessings of God. It has been the custom of generations to stand in this audience with God, envisioned as a transcendent, almighty King. For those who seek to emphasize an immanent spiritual dimension to life, it may seem more natural to sit. This siddur offers two versions of this multi-part prayer.

Blessing for Ancestral Wisdom

Every Rosh Hashanah of my childhood,
My father would ask my Bubbe,
"Why are your prayer book's pages folded over?"
Every year she answered him,
"This is where we cry."
From her life of wandering,
She understood tears and their stories:
In no way challenge fate
By failing to mention the One
Who watches overall,
But hope with 'the help of God,'
Be grateful with 'Praise God,' and 'Thank God.'

I also want to give thanks
For the good in my life and be amazed
By the wonders of the universe:
'With the help of the world,'
My tongue is getting used to new expressions.

Blessed are you, life-giving world,
Keeping us alive to learn from our ancestors.

בָּרוּךְ אַתָּה, עוֹלָם מְחַיֶּה, שֶׁהֶחֱיָינוּ לִלְמוֹד
מֵאֲבוֹתֵינוּ וּמֵאִמּוֹתֵינוּ.

*Baruch ata, olam m'chayeh,
shehechiyanu lilmod
mei-avoteinu umei-imoteinu.*

Blessing for Strength in the Face of Death

When I ask my friend how he's doing,
He answers me, 'Thank God,'
And he would respond thus
Even if he were suffering great distress.
I think, but don't respond to him:
Thanks, earth, from which I came at my birth.
During my life I have grown a sensitive soul,
But I expect to return to earth at my death
Without a soul and without pain,
Thanks to earth's embrace.

Blessed are you, generous Earth,
Embracing life and death.

בְּרוּכָה אַתְּ, תֵּבֵל נְדִיבָה,
הַמְחַבֶּקֶת חַיִּים וְמָוֶת.

*Bruchah at, teiveil n'divah,
ham'chabeket chayim v'mavet.*

Blessing for Holiness

Planet, world, universe:
Holy, holy, holy,
Surrounding and filling our lives.

תֵּבֵל, עוֹלָם, יְקוּם:
קָדוֹשׁ, קָדוֹשׁ, קָדוֹשׁ,
סוֹבֵב וּמְמַלֵּא אֶת חַיֵּינוּ.

Teiveil, olam, y'kum:
Kadosh, kadosh, kadosh,
Soveiv um'malei et chayeinu.

Blessed are you, holy and awesome cosmos.

בָּרוּךְ אַתָּה, יְקוּם קָדוֹשׁ וְנוֹרָא.

Baruch ata y'kum kadosh v'nora.

Blessing for Change

As the world changes
From season to season
So can we.
Every day let's ask ourselves
If we've been angry with those we love,
Been afraid to advocate for ourselves,
Forgiven as we want to be forgiven.

Blessed are you, ever-changing Earth,
Teacher of changes.

בְּרוּכָה אַתְּ, תֵּבֵל מִשְׁתַּנָה,
מוֹרַת הַשִּׁינוּיִם.

*Bruchah at, teiveil mishtanah,
morat hashinuyim.*

Blessing for Kindness

Our world is an emergency room
Where everyone will get a turn.
Until we get to the head of the line,
Let's be like the father who hugs
His silently suffering son,
Like the mother who speaks with her daughters
About the fears of violence that women endure,
Like the neighbor who pays attention
To his neighbor's complaint against the city,
And, even though he has heard it many times,
Listens with an open heart.

Blessed are you, united world,
Where kindness makes
Our connections steadfast.

בָּרוּךְ אַתָּה, עוֹלָם מְחוּבָּר,
הַמְכוֹנֵן קְשָׁרִים נֶאֱמָנִים לִגְמִילוּת חֲסָדִים.

*Baruch ata, olam m'chubar,
ham'chonen ksharim ne'emanim ligmilut chasadim.*

Blessing for Justice

If we pursue justice without tiring,
Give with an eye to justice,
Teach our children to do the same,
Then we've passed on what we inherited
In the short time we have.

Blessed is our tradition,
Paving a path to justice.

בְּרוּכָה מְסוֹרָתֵנוּ,
הַסוֹלֶלֶת דֶּרֶךְ לְצֶדֶק.

*Bruchah m'sorateinu
hasolelet derech l'tzedek.*

Blessing for Creatures: Birds

The woman who loves wetlands
Drives for hours to see birds
Swooping low over the marsh:
Egrets perching, heads aflame with sunlight,
Spoonbills swishing their long beaks,
Scooping fish into their gullets,
Pelicans flapping, landing, waiting.
Also waiting: the woman
Who looks for a flash
Of red and yellow stripes off a cattail,
For a streaky, dun-colored Immature
Learning to fish,
Or for an owl burrowing into its nest,
A vole in its talons,
Each one doing what it needs
To preserve itself and its kind.

Blessed are you, living world,
Delighting in every creature.

בְּרוּכָה אַתְּ, תֵּבֵל חַיָּה,
הַמְשַׁעֲשַׁעַת בְּכָל יְצוּר.

Bruchah at, teiveil chayah,
ham'sha-ashaat b'chol y'tzur.

Blessing for Prayer

Don't think there is no prayer
In a world without a master.
In Hebrew, to pray is a reflexive verb.
You need only yourself —
The 'I' that fears,
Makes people mad, and complains
And the 'I' that includes
All the 'I's in the world
And asks that you have compassion
On yourself
And on them all.

Blessed are you, self-sufficient world,
Praying to no master.

בְּרוּכָה אַתְּ, תֵּבֵל עַצְמָאִית,
שֶׁאֵינָהּ מִתְפַּלֶּלֶת לְאָדוֹן כָּלְשֶׁהוּ.

*Bruchah at, teiveil atzma-it,
she-einah mitpalelet laadon kolshehu.*

Blessing for Gratitude

What does it take to treasure each day,
To give thanks for the gifts not earned,
To savor the taste of every first fruit
And know that enough is as good as a feast?

It takes a lifetime to learn how to live,
To sort through the stuff that fills up our days,
To weigh and to measure just what to claim
And know that enough is as good as a feast.

Let's sit at nightfall with those we love
And light a candle to greet the dark,
Clasp our hands as we bless the bread
And know that enough is as good as a feast.

Let's open our hearts to the joy and the pain,
The bitter and sweet of the knowledge we've gained
And sweetly surrender to what we can't change
And know that enough is as good as a feast.
Blessed are you, abundant world,
Sharing your great goodness each day.

בָּרוּךְ אַתָּה, עוֹלָם מָלֵא,
הַמְחַלֵק אֶת רוֹב טוּבְךָ בְּכָל יוֹם תָּמִיד.

*Baruch ata, olam malei,
ham'chaleik et rov tuvcha
b'chol yom tamid.*

Blessing for Peace

This is my prayer and my path in life:
To betroth the world, so full,
To serve all others in joy,
To act towards each
With love and with truth,
And to trust
That right living and peace will bloom.

זֹאת תְּפִילָתִי וְדַרְכִּי בַּחַיִּים:
לְהִתְאָרֵס עִם הָעוֹלָם הַמָּלֵא,
לְשָׁרֵת אֲחֵרִים בְּשִׂמְחָה,
לְהִתְנַהֵג עִמָּם בְּחֶסֶד וּבֶאֱמֶת,
וְלִבְטוֹחַ שֶׁהַצֶּדֶק וְהַשָׁלוֹם יִפְרָחוּ.

Zot t'filati v'darki bachayim:
l'hitareis im ha-olam hamalei,
l'shareit acheirim b'simchah,
l'hitnaheig imam b'chesed uv'emet,
v'livto-ach shehatzedek v'hashalom yifr'chu.

Blessed are you, O singular world
Of wholeness and of peace.

בְּרוּכָה אַתְּ, תֵּבֵל יְחִידָה
שֶׁל שְׁלֵמוּת וְשָׁלוֹם.

Bruchah at, teiveil y'chidah
shel shleimut v'shalom.

Blessing for Jerusalem

Let us seek peace for Jerusalem.
Let us seek peace for a city open to all nations.
Let us seek peace for a city of wholeness and peace.
For all who love Jerusalem, let us speak only of peace.

Blessed are you, O City of Jerusalem,
whose name encompasses peace.

בְּרוּכָה אַתְּ, הָעִיר יְרוּשָׁלַיִם,
שֶׁהַשָּׁלוֹם כָּלוּל בִּשְׁמֵךְ.

*Bruchah at, ha'ir Y'rushalai-im,
she-hashalom kalul bishmech.*

The Amidah (II)

Blessing for Ancestral Wisdom

From my grandfather I inherited tefillin
And an old volume,
Walt Whitman's *Leaves of Grass*.
Mornings, I put on his tefillin
And read in his book,
"Why should I wish to see God
More than this day?
In the faces of men and women I see God
And in my own face in the mirror."
Like him, I know with every atom of my body
That all men and women
Are my brothers and sisters,
That my spirit is tied to the plants in the field
And to the far stars.

Blessed are you, life-giving world,
Keeping us alive to learn from our ancestors.

בָּרוּךְ אַתָּה, עוֹלָם מְחַיֶּה,
שֶׁהֶחֱיָינוּ לִלְמוֹד
מֵאֲבוֹתֵינוּ וּמֵאִמּוֹתֵינוּ.

*Baruch ata, olam m'chayeh,
shehecheyanu lilmod
mei-avoteinu umei-imoteinu.*

Blessing for Strength in the Face of Death

Death does not make me afraid.
By lifting the fallen, healing the sick,
Straightening those bent over,
Freeing those bound up,
We can live like heroes.

Blessed are you, world of tremendous forces
That intensify our own.

בְּרוּכָה אַתְּ, תֵּבֵל בַּעֲלַת כּוֹחוֹת עֲצוּמִים
שֶׁמַעֲצִימִים אֶת כּוֹחוֹתֵינוּ.

Bruchah at, teiveil
baalat kochot atzumim
shemaatzimim et kochoteinu.

Blessing for Holiness

Just as the lad Abram put a hammer
In the hand of the biggest idol
In his father's workshop,
Pointing to it as the one who
Shattered all the rest,
So our father Abraham
Put that self-same hammer
In our hands
That we might destroy images of God
That have screened us from seeing
There is nothing holier than the universe.

Blessed are you,
Holy and awesome cosmos!

בָּרוּךְ אַתָּה, יְקוּם קָדוֹשׁ וְנוֹרָא!

Baruch ata, y'kum kadosh v'nora!

Blessing for Change

There's no creature other than the human
Who looks in the mirror at the end of the day
To ask, "Have I done my best?"
There's no other creature that must
Look in the mirror at the end of each day.

Blessed are you, ever-changing world,
Teacher of changes.

בְּרוּכָה אַתְּ, תֵּבֵל מִשְׁתַּנָה,
מוֹרַת הַשִׁינוּיִם.

*Bruchah at, teiveil mishtanah,
morat hashinuyim.*

Blessing for Kindness

The world is broken and dangerous:
With lions roaming the streets,
It's much easier to stay at home.
Let us be blessed in this:
We will go out each day
We will see the wounded,
Hear their cries, respond.

Blessed are you, united world,
Where kindness makes
Our connections steadfast.

בָּרוּךְ אַתָּה, עוֹלָם מְחוּבַּר,
הַמְּכוֹנֵן קְשָׁרִים נֶאֱמָנִים
לִגְמִילוּת חֲסָדִים.

*Baruch ata, olam m'chubar,
ham'chonen ksharim ne'emanim
ligmilut chasadim*

Blessing for Justice

Justice—A staff, a promise, a target.
We trust in it, aim for it.
We build our fragile experiments
On the foundation of justice.

Blessed is our tradition,
Pushing us to pursue justice.

בְּרוּכָה מְסוֹרָתֵנוּ,
הַדוֹחֶפֶת אוֹתָנוּ לִרְדוֹף צֶדֶק.

*Bruchah m'sorateinu,
hadochefet otanu lirdof tzedek.*

Blessing for Creatures: Manatees

The huge gray manatees,
Ten-feet long, gentle, round-tailed giants,
Cousins of the elephants we feed at the zoo,
Bull and cow, all leathery, cavort in the creek,
Falling on one another in the water,
Spraying me and my neighbors,
Witnesses to this procreant power.
We forget for a moment
That the rotten run-off from our fields
Is killing the sea grasses that the manatees
Depend upon to live.

Blessed are you, living world,
Delighting in all your species.

בָּרוּךְ אַתָּה, עוֹלָם חַי,
הַמְשַׁעֲשֵׁעַ בְּכָל יְצוּר.

*Baruch ata, olam chai,
ham'shaashei-a b'chol y'tzur.*

Blessing for Prayer

When the world gives me words for song,
I am in the world, and the world is in me.
After many words and many songs,
There is no silence like the silence
After the song has been sung.

Blessed are you, noisy world,
Whose heavens pray silently.

בְּרוּכָה אַתְּ, תֵּבֵל רוֹעֶשֶׁת,
שֶׁשָּׁמַיִךְ מִתְפַּלְלִים בְּלִי מִלָה.

Bruchah at, teiveil ro'eshet,
sheshamayich mitpal'lim b'li milah.

Blessing for Gratitude

What can we do to treasure each day?
Give thanks for the gifts not earned,
Savor the taste of every first fruit
And know that enough is as good as a feast.

Blessed are you, world of abundance,
Showing us your great goodness each day.

בָּרוּךְ אַתָּה, עוֹלָם מָלֵא,
שֶׁמַרְאֶה אֶת רוֹב טוּבְךָ בְּכָל יוֹם תָּמִיד.

Baruch ata, olam malei,
shemareh et rov tuvcha
b'chol yom tamid.

Blessing for Peace

It is said
That students of the wise
Increase peace in the world.
If we are truly wise, then we are kind.
If kind, then at peace,
Sharing our peace with all.

Blessed are you, O singular world
Of wholeness and shalom.

בְּרוּכָה אַתְּ, תֵּבֵל יְחִידָה
שֶׁל שְׁלֵמוּת וְשָׁלוֹם.

Bruchah at, teiveil y'chidah
shel shleimut v'shalom.

Blessing for Jerusalem

Let us seek justice for a city open to all.
Let us seek justice for a city
made up of the hopes of every nation.
Let us seek justice for a city
whose prophets cried out for justice,
For they knew that without justice,
there is no joy, no ease,
no peace.

Blessed are you, O City of Jerusalem,
whose name encompasses peace.

בְּרוּכָה אַתְּ, הָעִיר יְרוּשָׁלַיִם,
שֶׁהַשָּׁלוֹם כָּלוּל בִּשְׁמֵךְ.

Bruchah at, ha'ir Y'rushalai-im,
shehashalom kalul bishmech.

Concluding the Service

Aleinu: It's on Us

It's on us to praise our Torah for saying,
"Love your neighbor as yourself."
It's on us to praise our prophets
For foreseeing a day
when those who dwell on earth
Shall beat their swords into plows
And learn war no more.
On that day, the world will be one.

עָלֵינוּ לְשַׁבֵּחַ אֶת תּוֹרָתֵנוּ
בְּאָמְרָהּ, 'וְאָהַבְתָּ לְרֵעֲךָ כָּמוֹךָ.'
עָלֵינוּ לְשַׁבֵּחַ אֶת נְבִיאֵינוּ
שֶׁחָזוּ יוֹם שֶׁבּוֹ יוֹשְׁבֵי תֵּבֵל
יְכַתְּתוּ חַרְבוֹתֵיהֶם לְאִתִּים
וְלֹא יִלְמְדוּ עוֹד מִלְחָמָה.
בַּיוֹם הַהוּא יִהְיֶה הָעוֹלָם אֶחָד.

Aleinu l'shabei-ach et Torateinu
b'omra, 'v'ahavta l'rei-acha kamocha.'
Aleinu l'shabei-ach et n'vi-einu
shechazu yom shebo yoshvei teiveil
y'chat't'tu charvoteihem l'itim
v'lo yilmidu od milchama.
Bayom hahu yih'yeh ha-olam echad.

Torah Service

Taking Out the Torah

Gates of righteousness, open for me,
That I may enter you.

פִּתְחוּ לִי שַׁעֲרֵי צֶדֶק,
אָבוֹא בָכֶם, אָבוֹא בָכֶם.

*Pitchu li shaarei tzedek,
avo vachem, avo vachem.*

(Psalm 118: 19, adapted)

Torah Blessings

Before reading, studying, or teaching Torah:
Blessed is our tradition for renewing Torah
In each generation.

בְּרוּכָה מְסוֹרָתֵנוּ שֶׁמְּחַדֶּשֶׁת תּוֹרָה בְּכָל דּוֹר.

Bruchah m'sorateinu
shem'chadeshet Torah b'chol dor.

After reading, studying, or teaching Torah:
Blessed is our tradition for envisioning Torah
As a refining fire.

בְּרוּכָה מְסוֹרָתֵנוּ שֶׁמְּדַמְיֶנֶת תּוֹרָה כְּאֵשׁ מְטַהֵר.

Bruchah m'sorateinu
shem'damyenet Torah k'eish m'taheir.

Returning the Torah

On Lifting the Torah:
This is the Torah that our tradition placed
Before the people of Israel,
According to the Scriptures,
In the name of Moses.

זֹאת הַתּוֹרָה
אֲשֶׁר שָׂמָה הַמְּסוֹרָה
לִפְנֵי בְּנֵי יִשְׂרָאֵל,
עַל פִּי הַמִּקְרָא,
בְּשֵׁם מֹשֶׁה.

Zot haTorah
asher samah ham'sorahh
lifnei v'nei Yisrael,
al pi hamikra
b'shem Moshe.

On Replacing the Torah:
She is a tree of life to all who hold fast to her
And all her supporters are happy.
Her ways are pleasant
And all her paths are peace.

עֵץ־חַיִּים הִיא לַמַּחֲזִיקִים בָּהּ
וְתֹמְכֶיהָ מְאֻשָּׁר.
דְּרָכֶיהָ דַרְכֵי־נֹעַם
וְכָל־נְתִיבוֹתֶיהָ שָׁלוֹם.

Aytz chaiyim hi, lamachazikim bah
v'tomchehah m'ushar;
Drachehah darchei-no'am
v'chol n'tivoteha shalom.
(Proverbs 3:18, 17)

This is the Torah

This is the Torah that was written
By human beings over many generations,
That Ezra is said to have put
Before the people of Israel
In the name of Moses,
That Hillel, the elder, summarized
Hundreds of years after Ezra:
"What is hateful to you,
Don't do to your fellow.
The rest is commentary."
That's worth studying.
Afterwards, do what needs doing.

Our ancestors were right when they said
that one mitzvah leads to another.
Likewise, a misdeed.
This I know from the mistakes of my life.
I don't believe in a commander,
But the language of 'Thou shalt' reminds me
That we inherited the mitzvot
To be refined like silver.

Blessed is our tradition
For envisioning Torah as a refining fire.

בְּרוּכָה מְסוֹרָתֵנוּ
שֶׁמְּדַמְיֶנֶת תּוֹרָה כְּאֵשׁ מְטַהֵר.

Bruchah m'sorateinu
shem'damyenet Torah
k'eish m'taheir.

Entering Shabbat and the Holy Days

Verses for Festive Song

1.

Be happy in your holiday and greatly rejoice!

וְשָׂמַחְתָּ בְּחַגֶּיךָ וְהָיִיתָ אַךְ שָׂמֵחַ!

*V'samachta b'chagecha
v'hayita ach samei-ach.*
(Deuteronomy 16: 14)

2.

Draw water in joy from the wells of fulfillment.

וּשְׁאַבְתֶּם מַיִם בְּשָׂשׂוֹן מִמַּעַיְנֵי הַיְשׁוּעָה.

*Ushavtem mayim bisason
mimay'-nei ha-y'shua.*
(Isaiah 12: 3)

3.

Let the heavens rejoice, let the earth be glad,
Let the sea and all its fullness thunder praise.

יִשְׂמְחוּ הַשָּׁמַיִם וְתָגֵל הָאָרֶץ,
יִרְעַם הַיָּם וּמְלוֹאוֹ.

Yism'chu hashamayim
V'tageil haaretz,
Yiram hayam um'lo-o.
(Psalm 96: 11)

4.

Light is sown for the righteous
And joy for the upright in heart.

אוֹר זָרֻעַ לַצַּדִּיק וּלְיִשְׁרֵי לֵב שִׂמְחָה.

Or zarua latzadik
ul'yishrei leiv simcha.
(Psalm 97: 11)

5.

The righteous flourish like a palm tree,
grow strong as a cedar of Lebanon.

צַדִּיק כַּתָּמָר יִפְרָח, כְּאֶרֶז בַּלְּבָנוֹן יִשְׂגֶּה.

Tsadik katamar yifrach,
k'erez bal'vanon yisgeh.
(Psalm 92, 13)

6.

Return, return, let us circle,
For our path has no end—
The chain is unbroken.
Our heart is one heart
From the distant past
To the distant future—
The chain is unbroken.

שׁוּבִי שׁוּבִי וְנָסוֹב,
כִּי דַרְכֵּנוּ אֵין לָהּ סוֹף—
כִּי עוֹד נִמְשֶׁכֶת הַשַּׁרְשֶׁרֶת.
וְלִבֵּנוּ לֵב אֶחָד
מֵעוֹלָם וְעֲדֵי עַד—
כִּי עוֹד נִמְשֶׁכֶת הַשַּׁרְשֶׁרֶת.

Shuvi shuvi v'nasov
ki darkeinu ein la sof—
ki od nimshechet hasharsheret.
V'libeinu leiv echad
mei-olam v'adei ad—
ki od nimshechet hasharsheret.
(Lyrics from "Rad HaLaila," Ya'akov Orland)

Blessings for Shabbat

Candle Lighting

Blessed is our wise tradition,
Inspiring us to light candles for Shabbat.
May our people and our world be blessed
With the light of hope and of peace.

בְּרוּכָה מְסוֹרַתֵנוּ הַנְּבוֹנָה
הַמְּעוֹרֶרֶת אוֹתָנוּ לְהַדְלִיק נֵר שֶׁל שַׁבָּת.
יְבוֹרַךְ עַמֵנוּ וְעוֹלָמֵנוּ
בְּאוֹר הַתִּקְוָה וְהַשָּׁלוֹם.

*Bruchah m'sorateinu hanvona
ha m'oreret otanu
l'hadlik neir shel Shabbat.
Y'vorach ameinu v'olameinu
b'or hatikvah v'hashalom.*

Kiddush

Blessed are you, fertile world,
Forming the fruit of the vine.
Blessed is our wise tradition,
Passing down to us the day of Shabbat,
First among our sacred assemblies
Calling to mind the beginning of all.
It is a day to stop for delight and for rest,
For freedom from work,
And for restoring the soul of our people.
So we lovingly welcome this Shabbat day.
Blessed are you, O holy Shabbat.

בְּרוּכָה אַתְּ, תֵּבֵל פּוֹרָה,
יוֹצֶרֶת פְּרִי הַגָּפֶן.
בְּרוּכָה מְסוֹרָתֵנוּ הַנְּבוֹנָה
הַמַּנְחִילָה לָנוּ אֶת יוֹם הַשַּׁבָּת,
רִאשׁוֹן הוּא לְמִקְרָאֵי קוֹדֶשׁ
זֵכֶר לְמַעֲשֵׂי בְרֵאשִׁית:
כִּי הוּא יוֹם שַׁבָּתוֹן
לְעֹנֶג וְלִמְנוּחָה,
לְחוֹפֶשׁ מֵעֲבוֹדָה,
וּלְהָשִׁיב אֶת נֶפֶשׁ הָאוּמָה.
אֶת יוֹם הַשַּׁבָּת הַזֶּה
בְּאַהֲבָה וּבְרָצוֹן נְקַבְּלָה.
בְּרוּכָה אַתְּ, שַׁבָּת קְדוֹשָׁה.

Bruchah at teiveil porah,
yotzeret p'ri hagafen.
Bruchah m'sorateinu hanvonah,
hamanchilah lanu
et yom haShabbat,
rishon hu l'mikra-ei kodesh
zeicher l'maasei v'reishit:
ki hu yom shabaton
l'oneg v'limnuchah,
l'chofesh mei-avodah,
ul' hashiv et nefesh ha-uma.
Et yom haShabbat hazeh
b'ahavah uv'ratzon n'kablah.
Bruchah at, Shabbat k'doshah.

Welcoming Shabbat

Come to us, come to us, holy Shabbat!
We waited for you all week,
Longing for the freedom that you bring;
Freely, we welcome you with love.

בּוֹאִי, בּוֹאִי, שַׁבַּת קְדוֹשָׁה!
חִכִּינוּ לָךְ שָׁבוּעַ שָׁלֵם,
קִוִּנוּ לַשִׁחְרוּר שֶׁאַת מְבִיאָה;
נְקַבְּלֵךְ בְּרָצוֹן וּבְאַהֲבָה.

Boi, boi, shabat k'dosha!
Chikinu lach shavua shaleim,
kivinu lashichrur she-at m'vi-a;
n'kableich b'ratzon uv'ahava.

Blessed are the candles lit in your honor.
Blessed is the fruit of the vine
Over which we say
To life, l'chaim!

בְּרוּכִים הַנֵּרוֹת שֶׁנִּדְלָקִים לִכְבוֹדֵךְ
וּבָרוּךְ פְּרִי הַגֶּפֶן
שֶׁנֹּאמַר עָלָיו לְחַיִּים!

Bruchim haneirot
shenidlakim l'chvodeich
u'varuch pri hagefen
shenomar alav l'chayim!

For Shabbat: An Added Soul

Better to grow two souls than just one:
One with a shell for weekdays,
Another for Shabbat,
A soft, quiet bird that seeks its food
Without chasing away the other birds.
That small bird lands
And flutters in my heart:
My skin sheds,
Fins and a breathing hole appear,
I dive to swim among the dolphins.

Blessed is our tradition
For making Shabbat holy.

בְּרוּכָה מְסוֹרָתֵנוּ,
מְקַדֶּשֶׁת הַשַׁבָּת.

*Bruchah m'sorateinu,
m'kadeshet haShabbat.*

The Stars Come Out: Havdalah Suite

1.

Flickering light above our heads,
Sweetness of cinnamon,
Sharp pungency of cloves,
Hiss of candle plunged in wine,
Shred of smoke:
Havdalah.

2.

My great grandfather used to dip his finger
Into the remnants of the wine
And dab it into the corner of his eye
And into his pants' pocket
So he might see good fortune
In the coming week.
What remains? The refrain of an old song:
"May our descendants and our coins
Be as numerous as the sand on the shore
And the stars in the night sky."

3.

When we fill a cup of wine to its brim
And share spices
We savor the sweetness of Shabbat
One last time.

When we light a braided candle,
A door opens to the week
Where we see everything
by at least two lights or more.

When we wish each other a good week,
We are already longing
For the light
Of the Shabbat to come.

So we bless the fruit of the vine,
The blended spices,
The braided light,
And distinguish
Between the holiness of Shabbat
And the workaday week.

Together, we sing:
A good week,
A week of joy,
A week of peace.

נָשִׁיר בְּיַחַד:
שָׁבוּעַ טוֹב,
שְׁבוּעַת שִׂמְחָה,
שְׁבוּעַת שָׁלוֹם.

Nashir b'yachad:
shavua tov,
sh'vuat simchah,
sh'vuat shalom.

Candle Lighting for Rosh Hashanah

Blessed is our wise tradition,
Inspiring us to light candles for
(*On Friday night, add:* Shabbat and)
This Day of Remembrance.
May our people and our world be blessed
With the light of hope and of peace.

בְּרוּכָה מְסוֹרָתֵנוּ הַנְּבוֹנָה,
הַמְּעוֹרֶרֶת אוֹתָנוּ לְהַדְלִיק נֵר שֶׁל
(שַׁבָּת וְ)
יוֹם הַזִּכָּרוֹן.
יְבוֹרַךְ עַמֵּנוּ וְעוֹלָמֵנוּ בְּאוֹר הַתִּקְוָה וְהַשָּׁלוֹם.

Bruchah m'sorateinu hanvonah
ham'oreret otanu l'hadlik neir shel
(Shabbat v')
Yom haZikaron.
Y'vorach ameinu v'olameinu
B'or hatikvah v'hashalom.

Kiddush for Rosh Hashanah

Blessed are you, fertile world,
Forming the fruit of the vine.
Blessed is our wise tradition,
Passing down to us
(*on Friday nights, add:* Sabbaths for rest and)
Days of Awe for holiness
At the renewal of the year:
This Day of Remembrance
To marvel at the wondrous birth of the universe,
To contemplate the year that has passed,
And to awaken to the cries of the Shofar.
So we lovingly welcome
This Rosh Hashanah day.

Blessed are you, living world,
That has kept us alive, sustained us
And allowed us to reach this moment.

בְּרוּכָה אַתְּ, תֵּבֵל פּוֹרָה,
יוֹצֶרֶת פְּרִי הַגָּפֶן.
בְּרוּכָה מְסוֹרָתֵנוּ הַנְּבוֹנָה
הַמַּנְחִילָה לָנוּ
(שַׁבָּתוֹת לִמְנוּחָה וְ)
יָמִים נוֹרָאִים לִקְדוּשָׁה
בְּמוֹעֵד הִתְחַדְּשׁוּת הַשָּׁנָה:
הַיּוֹם הַזִּכָּרוֹן הַזֶּה אֶת
לְהִתְפַּלֵּא מֵלֵידַת הַיְקוּם הַנִּפְלָא,
לְהַרְהֵר עַל הַשָּׁנָה שֶׁעָבְרָה,
וְלְהִתְעוֹרֵר מִקּוֹלוֹת הַשּׁוֹפָר.

(אֶת יוֹם הַשַׁבָּת הַזֶּה וְ)
אֶת יוֹם הַזִּכָּרוֹן הַזֶּה,
בְּאַהֲבָה וּבְרָצוֹן נְקַבְּלָה.

בָּרוּךְ אַתָּה, עוֹלָם חַי,
שֶׁהֶחֱיָנוּ, וְקִיְּמָנוּ, וְהִגִּיעָנוּ לַזְּמַן הַזֶּה.

Bruchah at teiveil porah,
yotzeret p'ri hagafen.
Bruchah m'sorateinu hanvonah
hamanchilah lanu
(shabatot limnuchah)
yomim noraim lik'dushah
b'mo-eid hitchadshut hashana:
et Yom haZikaron hazeh
l'hitpale mileidat hay'kum hanifla,
l'harheir al hashanah she-avrah,
vil'hitoreir mikolot hashofar.
(Et yom haShabbat hazeh v')
Et Yom HaZikaron hazeh
b'ahavah uv'ratzon n'kablah.

Baruch ata olam chai,
shehecheyanu, v'kiy'manu,
v'higi-anu laz'man hazeh.

For Rosh haShanah: Tashlich Poem

I lead my grandchildren to the riverbank,
Ask them to ponder what would they like to change.
Mostly they want to change their brother or sister.
That being the case, the best thing
Is to eat apples with honey on our lips,
And to give thanks
For the sweetness of second chances,
Even if we don't always take them.

Blessed is our tradition,
Tasting sweetness
At the season of the new year.

בְּרוּכָה מְסוֹרָתֵנוּ
הַטוֹעֶמֶת אֶת הַמָּתוֹק
בְּמוֹעֵד הַשָׁנָה.

*Bruchah m'sorateinu
hato-emet et hamatok
bamo-eid hashanah.*

Candle Lighting for Yom Kippur

Blessed is our wise tradition,
Inspiring us to light candles for
(*on Friday night, add:* Shabbat and)
The Day of Atonement.
May our people and our world be blessed
With the light of hope and of peace.

בְּרוּכָה מְסוֹרָתֵנוּ הַנְּבוֹנָה,
הַמְּעוֹרֶרֶת אוֹתָנוּ לְהַדְלִיק נֵר שֶׁל
(שַׁבַּת וְ)
יוֹם הַכִּפּוּרִים.
יְבוֹרַךְ עַמֵּנוּ וְעוֹלָמֵנוּ בְּאוֹר הַתִּקְוָה וְהַשָּׁלוֹם.

*Bruchah m'sorateinu hanvonah
ham'oreret otanu l'hadlik neir shel
(Shabbat vi-)
Yom haKipurim.
Yevorach ameinu v'olameinu
b'or hatikvah v'hashalom.*

Blessed are you, living world,
That has kept us alive, sustained us
And allowed us to reach this moment.

בָּרוּךְ אַתָּה, עוֹלָם חַי,
שֶׁהֶחֱיָנוּ, וְקִיְּמָנוּ, וְהִגִּיעָנוּ לַזְּמַן הַזֶּה.

Baruch ata, olam chai,
shehecheyanu v'kiy'manu
v'higi-anu laz'man hazeh.

For Yom Kippur: Self-Correction

1.

From evening to morning to evening
The world revolves.
Nature self-corrects, but will I?
There's much to atone for
In how I manage my world,
Even if there's no book
In which all my deeds are written.

2.

No law, nor judge, said Cain in his heart
And killed his brother to test his claim.
Cain was asked, where are you?
I too check whether I am bent or upright.

3.

Difficult to be a sheep without a shepherd,
David said in his heart,
so prayed to a god to guide him.
To forge a soul is work suited to a lonely shepherd:
I am the only sheep that I can guide.

4.

It is said that Abraham, during his wanderings,
Planted a tamarisk and asked it many questions.
I try to live without answers:
That's the legacy that I leave my children.

Blessed is our tradition,
Deepening how we take stock
And turn ourselves around.

בְּרוּכָה מְסוֹרָתֵנוּ
הַמַעֲמִיקָה אֶת חֶשְׁבּוֹן נַפְשֵׁנוּ
וְחַזָרָתֵנוּ בִּתְשׁוּבָה.

*Bruchah m'sorateinu,
hamaamikah et cheshbon nafsheinu
v'chazarateinu bit'shuvah.*

Candle Lighting for Sukkot

Blessed is our wise tradition,
Inspiring us to light candles for
(*On Fridays add:* Shabbat and)
This special day.
May our people and our world be blessed
With the light of hope and peace.

בְּרוּכָה מְסוֹרָתֵנוּ הַנְּבוֹנָה
הַמְּעוֹרֶרֶת אוֹתָנוּ לְהַדְלִיק נֵר שֶׁל
(שַׁבַּת וְ)
יוֹם טוֹב.
יְבוֹרַךְ עַמֵנוּ וְעוֹלָמֵנוּ בְּאוֹר הַתִּקְוָה וְהַשָּׁלוֹם.

*Bruchah m'sorateinu hanvonah,
ham'oreret otanu l'hadlik neir shel
(Shabbat vi-)
Yom tov.
Y'vorach ameinu v'olameinu
B'or hatikvah v'hashalom.*

Kiddush for Sukkot

Blessed are you, fertile world,
Forming the fruit of the vine.
Blessed is our wise tradition,
Passing down to us this
(*on Friday night, add:* Sabbaths for rest and)
Festivals for joy:
This holiday of Sukkot,
A time to gather in our harvest,
A time to dwell in fragile shelters,
And a time to rejoice.
We lovingly welcome
(*On Friday night, add:* this Shabbat day and)
This holiday of Sukkot.

Blessed are you, living world,
That has kept us alive, sustained us
And allowed us to reach this moment.

בְּרוּכָה אַתְּ, תֵּבֵל פּוֹרָה,
יוֹצֶרֶת פְּרִי הַגָּפֶן.
בְּרוּכָה מְסוֹרַתֵנוּ הַנְּבוֹנָה
הַמַּנְחִילָה לָנוּ
(שַׁבָּתוֹת לִמְנוּחָה וְ)
חַגִּים וּזְמַנִּים לְשָׂשׂוֹן:
אֶת חַג הַסֻּכּוֹת הַזֶּה,
זְמַן לִקְצוֹר וְלֶאֱסוֹף,
זְמַן לָדוּר בְּסֻכּוֹת,
וּזְמַן לִשְׂמוֹחַ.

(אֶת יוֹם הַשַּׁבָּת הַזֶּה וְ)
אֶת חַג הַסֻּכּוֹת הַזֶּה
בְּאַהֲבָה וּבְרָצוֹן נְקַבְּלָה.

בָּרוּךְ אַתָּה, עוֹלָם חַי,
שֶׁהֶחֱיָנוּ, וְקִיְּמָנוּ, וְהִגִּיעָנוּ לַזְּמַן הַזֶּה.

Bruchah at, teiveil porah,
yotzeret p'ri hagafen.
Bruchah m'sorateinu hanvonah
hamanchilah lanu
(shabatot lim'nuchah)
chagim uz'manim l'sason:
et chag haSukkot hazeh,
z'man liktsor v'le-esof,
z'man ladur ba-sukkot,
uz'man lismo-ach.
(Et yom haShabbat hazeh v')
Et chag haSukkot hazeh
b'ahavah uv'ratzon n'kablah.
Baruch ata, olam chai,
shehecheyanu, v'kiy'manu
v'higi-anu laz'man hazeh.

Blessing in the Sukkah

Blessed is our wise tradition,
Inspiring us to dwell in a Sukkah.

בְּרוּכָה מְסוֹרָתֵנוּ הַנְבוֹנָה
הַמִתְעוֹרֶרֶת אוֹתָנוּ לָדוּר בַּסוּכּוֹת.

*Bruchah m'sorateinu hanvonah
hamitoreret otanu
ladur basukkot.*

Blessings on Taking the Four Species

Blessed are you, fertile earth,
Growing the four species
That we wave on this holiday of Sukkot.

בְּרוּכָה אַתְּ, תֵּבֵל פּוֹרָה,
הַמַצְמִיחָה אֶת אַרְבַּעַת הַמִּינִים
שֶׁאֲנַחְנוּ מְנַפְנְפִים בְּחַג הַסוּכּוֹת.

*Bruchah at, teiveil porah,
hamatzmichah et arbaat haminim
sheanachnu m'naf-n'fim
b'chag ha-Sukkot.*

A Sukkot Request

We have spread a roof of branches over us,
Invited to our Sukkah dear friends,
Spoken of the holiday and its symbols,
Knowing that this tiny, flimsy house
Will comfort us only for a few days
Before the coming of the rains
And the devouring winds.
So let us praise the shade
Beneath which we rest
And pray that we merit spending
Eight such days another year.

Blessed is our tradition,
Celebrating a festival
Of fragile happiness.

בְּרוּכָה מְסוֹרָתֵנוּ,
הַחוֹגֶגֶת חַג לְשִׂמְחָה שַׁבִירִית.

*Bruchah m'sorateinu
hachogeget chag
l'simcha shavirit.*

Candle Lighting for Shemini Atzeret–Simchat Torah

Blessed is our wise tradition,
Inspiring us to light candles for
(*On Friday night add:* Shabbat and)
This special day.
May our people and our world be blessed
With the light of hope and peace.

בְּרוּכָה אַתְּ, מְסוֹרַתֵנוּ הַנְּבוֹנָה,
הַמְּעוֹרֶרֶת אוֹתָנוּ לְהַדְלִיק נֵר שֶׁל
(שַׁבָּת וְ)
יוֹם טוֹב.
יְבוֹרַךְ עַמֵּנוּ וְעוֹלָמֵנוּ בְּאוֹר הַתִּקְוָה וְהַשָּׁלוֹם.

Bruchah m'sorateinu hanvonah
ham'oreret otanu l'hadlik neir shel
(Shabbat v')
Yom tov.
Y'vorach ameinu v'olameinu
b'or hatikvah v'hashalom.

Kiddush for Shemini Atzeret–Simchat Torah

Blessed are you, fertile world,
Forming the fruit of the vine.
Blessed is our wise tradition,
Passing down to us
(*on Friday night, add:* Sabbaths for rest and)
Festivals for joy:
This special day of assembling,
A time for tasting our goodly portion,
A time for delighting our lovely inheritance,
And a time for rejoicing in Jewish learning.
We lovingly welcome
(*On Friday night, add:* This Shabbat and)
This Shemini Atzeret–Simchat Torah.

Blessed are you, living world,
That has kept us alive, sustained us
And allowed us to reach this moment.

בְּרוּכָה אַתְּ, תֵּבֵל פּוֹרָה,
יוֹצֶרֶת פְּרִי הַגֶּפֶן.
בְּרוּכָה מְסוֹרַתֵנוּ הַנְּבוֹנָה
הַמַּנְחִילָה לָנוּ
(שַׁבָּתוֹת לִמְנוּחָה וְ)
חַגִּים וּזְמַנִּים לְשָׂשׂוֹן:
אֶת שְׁמִינִי חַג הָעֲצֶרֶת הַזֶּה,
זְמַן לִטְעוֹם מִטּוּב חֶלְקֵנוּ,
זְמַן לְשַׁעֲשֵׁעַ בְּיוֹפִי יְרוּשָׁתֵנוּ,

וּזְמַן לִשְׂמוֹחַ בְּעוֹנֶג תּוֹרָתֵנוּ.
(אֶת יוֹם הַשַּׁבָּת הַזֶּה וְ)
אֶת שְׁמִינִי חַג הָעֲצֶרֶת הַזֶּה
בְּאַהֲבָה וּבְרָצוֹן נְקַבְּלָה.

בְּרוּכָה אַתָּה, עוֹלָם חַי,
שֶׁהֶחֱיָנוּ, וְקִיְּמָנוּ, וְהִגִּיעָנוּ לַזְּמַן הַזֶּה.

Bruchah at, teiveil porah,
yotzeret p'ri hagafen.
Bruchah m'sorateinu hanvonah
hamanchilah lanu
(shabatot limnuchah)
chagim uz'manim l'sason:
et Shimini chag haAtzeret hazeh,
z'man litom mituv chelkeinu,
z'man l'shaashay-a b'yofi y'rushateinu,
uz'man lismo-ach b'torateinu.
(Et yom haShabat hazeh v')
Et Shimini chag haAtzeret hazeh
b'ahavah uv'ratzon n'kablah

Baruch ata, olam chai,
shehecheyanu v'kiy'manu
v'higi-anu laz'man hazeh.

My Song for Simchat Torah

In my youth, my father brought me
To dance with the Torah at a Hasidic shtiebel.
As an adult, I danced with the Torah
as a Hasid aflame
To show the children of my synagogue
How to dance with the Torah with one's heart aflame.
In old age, I've learned
that it's necessary to dance with the Torah
Strangely and wondrously,
For if one doesn't make the Torah new
Can it be made holy?

Blessed is our tradition,
Always learning to make itself new.

בְּרוּכָה מְסוֹרָתֵנוּ
שֶׁתָּמִיד מִתְחַדֶּשֶׁת בְּשִׂמְחָה.

*Bruchah m'sorateinu
shetamid mitchadeshet
b'simchah.*

Blessings for Chanukah

Blessed is our wise tradition,
So full of light and joy,
Inspiring us to light the candles of Chanukah.

בְּרוּכָה מְסוֹרַתֵנוּ הַנְּבוֹנָה,
מְסוֹרָה שֶׁל אוֹרָה וְשִׂמְחָה,
הַמְעוֹרֶרֶת אוֹתָנוּ לְהַדְלִיק נֵר שֶׁל חֲנוּכָּה.

Bruchah m'sorateinu hanvonah,
m'sorah shel orah v'simchah,
ham'oreret otanu
l'hadlik neir shel Chanukah.

Blessed is our wise tradition,
So full of light and joy,
Inspiring us to great deeds at this time.

בְּרוּכָה מְסוֹרַתֵנוּ הַנְּבוֹנָה
מְסוֹרָה שֶׁל אוֹרָה וְשִׂמְחָה,
הַמְעוֹרֶרֶת אוֹתָנוּ לְמַעֲשִׂים גְּדוֹלִים בַּזְּמַן הַזֶּה.

Bruchah m'sorateinu hanvonah,
m'sorah shel orah v'simchah,
ham'oreret otanu
l'maasim g'dolim baz'man hazeh.

Add on the first night:
Blessed are you, living world,
Vast and awesome universe,
That has kept us alive, sustained us
And allowed us to reach this moment.

בָּרוּךְ אַתָּה, עוֹלָם חַי,
יְקוּם עָצוּם וְנוֹרָא,
שֶׁהֶחֱיָנוּ, וְקִיְּמָנוּ, וְהִגִּיעָנוּ לַזְּמַן הַזֶּה.

Baruch ata, olam chai,
y'kum atzum v'nora,
shehecheyanu v'kiy'manu
v'higi-anu laz'man hazeh.

Meditation before the Chanukah Candles

At a great distance from wondrous miracles,
I sit and watch the tiny candles
Burning in my deep diasporah,
Competing with their small light
Against the giant blaze of Christmas,
Feeling grateful for a festival of small lights,
Because only from small actions—
Giving a soft answer,
Turning away anger,
Increasing peace at home—
Is the world sustained.

Blessed is our tradition,
Dedicating small candles to great deeds.

בְּרוּכָה מְסוֹרָתֵנוּ
הַמְקַדֶּשֶׁת אוּרִים קְטַנִּים לְמַעֲשִׂים גְּדוֹלִים.

*Bruchah m'sorateinuo
ham'kadeshet urim k'tanim
l'maasim g'dolim.*

For Tu B'Shvat: Change Is Like That

The full moon of Sh'vat
Appears in the dark heaven.
Despite the cold outside,
The first warmth of spring
Flows up the trees.
This happens without our seeing it.
Change is like that.

Blessed is our tradition,
Paying attention to life's flow.

בְּרוּכָה מְסוֹרָתֵנוּ
שֶׁשָּׂמָה לֵב לַחַיִּים הַזּוֹרְמִים.

*Bruchah m'sorateinu
shesama leiv
lachayim hazormim.*

For Purim: Dress Rehearsal

Which one is Haman?
Who is Mordecai?
On all other nights there is no question:
On this night, it's essential to know
That there's a Mordecai in every Haman
And a Haman in every Mordecai,
That both thirst for the blood of their enemies
And do kindness to those they love.

Blessed is our tradition,
For playing with the enemy.

בְּרוּכָה מְסוֹרָתֵנוּ
שֶׁמְשַׂחֶקֶת עִם הָאוֹיֵב.

*Bruchah m'sorateinu
shem'sacheket im ha-oyeiv.*

Candle Lighting for Passover

Blessed is our wise tradition,
Inspiring us to light candles for
(*on Friday night, add:* Shabbat and
This special day.
May our people and our world be blessed
With the light of hope and of peace.

בְּרוּכָה מְסוֹרָתֵנוּ הַנְּבוֹנָה
הַמְּעוֹרֶרֶת אוֹתָנוּ לְהַדְלִיק נֵר שֶׁל
(שַׁבָּת וְ)
יוֹם טוֹב.
יְבוֹרַךְ עַמֵּנוּ וְעוֹלָמֵנוּ בְּאוֹר הַתִּקְוָה וְהַשָּׁלוֹם.

Bruchah m'sorateinu hanvonah,
ham'oreret otanu l'hadlik neir shel
(Sha-bat v')
Yom tov.
Y'vorach ameinu v'olameinu
b'or hatikvah v'hashalom.

Kiddush for Passover

Blessed are you, fertile world,
Forming the fruit of the vine.
Blessed is our wise tradition,
Passing down to us
(*on Friday nights, add:* Sabbaths for rest and)
Festivals for joy:
This holiday of Matzot,
A time for telling of our people's origin,
A time for leaving our own enslavement,
And a time for claiming freedom
For all who dwell on Earth.
We lovingly welcome
(This Shabbat day and)
This Passover holiday.

Blessed are you, living world,
That has kept us alive, sustained us
And allowed us to reach this moment.

בְּרוּכָה אַתְּ, תֵּבֵל פּוֹרָה,
יוֹצֶרֶת פְּרִי הַגָּפֶן.
בְּרוּכָה מְסוֹרָתֵנוּ הַנְּבוֹנָה
הַמַּנְחִילָה לָנוּ
(שַׁבָּתוֹת לִמְנוּחָה וְ)
חַגִּים וּזְמַנִּים לְשָׂשׂוֹן:
חַג הַמַּצּוֹת הַזֶּה, אֶת
זְמַן לְסַפֵּר עַל מוֹצָא עַמֵּנוּ,
זְמַן לָצֵאת מֵעַבְדוּתֵנוּ,

וּזְמַן לִטְעוֹן חֵרוּת לְכָל יוֹשְׁבֵי תֵּבֵלֵנוּ.
(אֶת יוֹם הַשַּׁבָּת הַזֶּה וְ)
אֶת חַג הַמַּצּוֹת הַזֶּה
בְּאַהֲבָה וּבְרָצוֹן נְקַבְּלָה.

בָּרוּךְ אַתָּה, עוֹלָם חַי,
שֶׁהֶחֱיָנוּ, וְקִיְּמָנוּ, וְהִגִּיעָנוּ לַזְּמַן הַזֶּה.

Bruchah at, teiveil porah,
yotzeret p'ri hagafen.
Bruchah m'sorateinu hanvonah
hamanchilah lanu
(shabatot limnuchah v')
chagim u'zmanim l'sason:
et chag ha-Matzot hazeh,
z'man l'sapeir al motza ameinu,
z'man latzeit mei-avduteinu,
uz'man liton cheirut l'chol yoshvei teiveileinu.
(Et yom ha-Shabbat hazeh v')
Et chag haMatzot hazeh
b'ahavah u'vratson n'kab'lah.

Baruch ata, olam chai,
shehecheyanu v'kiy'manu
v'higi-anu laz'man hazeh.

For Passover: A Hymn to Diasporah

From across the sea,
They brought their heavy utensils,
The brass mortar and pestle,
Reminding them of familiar spices,
Cinnamon, cloves, and chopped nuts,
Expected nothing from these gentiles
Among whom they peddled
To earn their living,
Would never trust them,
Never believe that one day,
Their great-grandchildren would marry them,
Invite them to chop nuts
In Bubbe's mortar and pestle,
Light holiday candles with them,
Open their doors to walk with them out of Egypt
In love.

Blessed is our tradition,
Celebrating our redemption in love.

בְּרוּכָה מְסוֹרָתֵנוּ,
הַחוֹגֶגֶת אֶת גְּאוּלָתֵנוּ בְּאַהֲבָה.

*Bruchah m'sorateinu
hachogeget et g'ulateinu
b'ahavah.*

Candle Lighting
for the Seventh Night of Passover

Blessed is our wise tradition,
Inspiring us to light candles for
(*On Friday night, add:* Shabbat and)
This special day.
May our people and our world be blessed
With the light of hope and of peace.

בְּרוּכָה מְסוֹרָתֵנוּ הַנְּבוֹנָה,
הַמְּעוֹרֶרֶת אוֹתָנוּ לְהַדְלִיק נֵר שֶׁל
(שַׁבָּת וְ)
יוֹם טוֹב.
יְבוֹרַךְ עַמֵּנוּ וְעוֹלָמֵנוּ בְּאוֹר הַתִּקְוָה וְהַשָּׁלוֹם.

*Bruchah m'sorateinu hanvonah,
ham'oreret otanu l'hadlik neir shel
(Shabat v')
Yom tov.
Y'vorach ameinu v'olameinu
b'or hatikvah v'hashalom.*

Kiddush
for the Seventh Night of Passover

Blessed are you, fertile world,
Forming the fruit of the vine.
Blessed is our wise tradition,
Passing down to us
(*on Friday nights, add:* Sabbaths for rest and)
Festivals for joy:
This holiday of Matzot,
A time for crossing through our straits,
A time for drawing close to our beloveds,
And a time for enjoying our freedom.
We lovingly welcome
(*on Friday nights, add:* This Shabbat day and)
This seventh day of Passover.

Blessed are you, living world,
That has kept us alive, sustained us
And allowed us to reach this moment.

בְּרוּכָה אַתְּ, תֵּבֵל פּוֹרָה,
יוֹצֶרֶת פְּרִי הַגָּפֶן.
בְּרוּכָה מְסוֹרָתֵנוּ הַנְּבוֹנָה
הַמַּנְחִילָה לָנוּ
(שַׁבָּתוֹת לִמְנוּחָה וְ)
חַגִּים וּזְמַנִּים לְשָׂשׂוֹן:
אֶת חַג הַמַּצּוֹת הַזֶּה,
זְמַן לַעֲבוֹר אֶת מֵצָרֵינוּ,
זְמַן לְקָרֵב לְאֲהוּבֵינוּ,

וּזְמַן לְהִתְעַנֵּג בְּחֵרוּתֵנוּ.
(אֶת יוֹם הַשַּׁבָּת הַזֶּה וְ)
אֶת יוֹם הַשְּׁבִיעִי שֶׁל פֶּסַח הַזֶּה
בְּאַהֲבָה וּבְרָצוֹן נְקַבְּלָה.

בָּרוּךְ אַתָּה, עוֹלָם חַי,
שֶׁהֶחֱיָנוּ, וְקִיְּמָנוּ, וְהִגִּיעָנוּ לַזְּמַן הַזֶּה.

Bruchah at, teiveil porah,
yotzeret p'ri hagafen.
Bruchah m'sorateinu hanvonah,
hamanchilah lanu
(shabatot lim'nucha v')
chagim u'zmanim l'sason:
et yom hash'vi-i shel Pesach hazeh,
z'man laavor et meitzareinu,
z'man likareiv l'ahuveinu,
z'man l'hitaneig b'cheiruteinu.
(Et yom haShabbat hazeh v')
Et hashvi-i shel Pesach hazeh
b'ahavah u'vratzon n'kab'la.

Baruch ata, olam chai,
shehecheyanu v'kiy'manu
v'higi-anu laz'man hazeh.

Songs from The Song of Songs

1.

I am my beloved's and my beloved,
The shepherd among the roses, is mine.
Who is this coming up from the desert,
Who is coming
Spiced with myrrh and frankincense,
Myrrh and frankincense?
I am my beloved's and my beloved,
The shepherd among the roses, is mine.
You have captured my heart, O my sister,
My bride, you have captured me.
Awake, O north wind,
Come, O south wind!
I am my beloved's and my beloved,
The shepherd among the roses, is mine.

דּוֹדִי לִי וַאֲנִי לוֹ הָרוֹעֶה בַּשׁוֹשַׁנִּים.
מִי זֹאת עוֹלָה מִן הַמִּדְבָּר, מִי זֹאת עוֹלָה,
מְקֻטֶּרֶת מוֹר, מוֹר וּלְבוֹנָה, מוֹר וּלְבוֹנָה?
דּוֹדִי לִי וַאֲנִי לוֹ, הָרוֹעֶה בַּשׁוֹשַׁנִּים.
לִבַּבְתִּנִי אֲחוֹתִי כַלָּה, לִבַּבְתִּנִי כַלָּה.(2x)
דּוֹדִי לִי וַאֲנִי לוֹ, הָרוֹעֶה בַּשׁוֹשַׁנִּים.
עוּרִי צָפוֹן וּבוֹאִי תֵימָן. (2x)
דּוֹדִי לִי וַאֲנִי לוֹ, הָרוֹעֶה בַּשׁוֹשַׁנִּים.

Dodi li vaani lo, haro-eh bashoshanim.
Mi zot olah min hamidbar, mi zot olah,

m'kuteret mor, mor ul'vonah, mor ul'vonah?
Dodi li vaani lo, haro-eh bashoshanim.
Livavtini achoti kalah, livavtini kalah (2x).
Dodi li vaani lo, haro-eh bashoshanim (2x).
(Song of Songs 2:6, 3:16, 4:9, 4:16)

2.

I have come down to the nut garden
To look among the reeds of the river
To see if the vine has flowered,
If the pomegranates are in bud.
Come, my beloved, let's go out to the field,
We'll sleep in the villages,
We'll wake among the vineyards,
We'll see if the vine has flowered,
Its blossoms formed.

אֶל גִּנַּת אֱגוֹז יָרַדְתִּי
לִרְאוֹת בְּאִבֵּי הַנָּחַל
לִרְאוֹת הֲפָרְחָה הַגֶּפֶן,
הֵנֵצוּ הָרִמּוֹנִים.
לְכָה דוֹדִי נֵצֵא הַשָּׂדֶה,
נָלִינָה בַּכְּפָרִים,
נַשְׁכִּימָה לַכְּרָמִים,
נִרְאֶה אִם פָּרְחָה הַגֶּפֶן,
פִּתַּח הַסְּמָדַר.

*El ginat egoz yarad'ti
lirot b'i-bei hanachal*

lirot haparchah hagefen,
heineitzu harimonim.
L'cha dodi neitzei hasadeh,
nalinah bak'farim,
nashkimah lak'ramim,
nireh im parchah hagefen,
pitach has'madar.
(Song of Songs 6:11, 7:12-13)

3.

I am opening to you, my beloved.
(Will you open, open to me?)

קַמְתִּי אֲנִי לִפְתּוֹחַ לְדוֹדִי.

Kamti ani lifto-ach l'dodi.
(Song of Songs 5:5)

4.

Oh, you are fair my darling,
Oh you are fair.

הִנָּךְ יָפָה רַעְיָתִי, הִנָּךְ יָפָה.

Hinach yafah raayati
hinach yafah.
(Song of Songs 1:15)

For Yom HaShoah and Yom HaZikaron: To Remember and to Blot Out

On the days of remembrance—
A feeling
That there is no suffering
Like our suffering:
I buy a pen, write on a clean sheet of paper
Amalek–Haman–Chmelnitzki–Hitler–Hamas,
Attack the names with a sharp line
To blot out their memory,
But not so much that I forget.

May our people be blessed
As we remember our losses.

יְבוֹרַךְ עַמֵּנוּ
בְּזָכְרֵנוּ אֶת אֵלֶּה שֶׁאִבַּדְנוּ.

Y'vorach ameinu
b'zochreinu
et eileh she-ibadnu.

For Israel's Independence Day: All in the Family

1.

We sat, my brother and I, in the backseat
And quarreled unceasingly,
Until our mother, may she rest in peace, asked,
'How will there be peace in the world,
If two brothers cannot live together in peace?'
We knew from the Torah stories she taught us
That Cain killed his brother Hevel out of jealousy,
That Jacob stole and Esav was ready to murder
To receive what he could never get,
The indivisible blessing.

Nowadays my brother and I
Meet for meals on our birthdays,
Talk of our cholesterol levels and sleep apnea,
Of the kids' jobs
And of the Israelis and Palestinians,
He, embarrassed, like a diasporah Jew, and I, shaken
By this quarrel of brothers
Who rise from their graves like ghosts
To deceive and to fight, to die and to kill,
United only by their family plot
Where they pause
To bury their dead.

2.

The Palestinians commemorate
Their tragic Naqba,
A holy day of remembering
And mourning the loss of their nation.
When the day comes that they celebrate
The beginning of their state, I suggest
That they celebrate a Palestinian Purim,
With costumes, masks, and hashish
(The Muslims won't be drinking alcohol),
When they'll wipe out
The name of Israel once a year,
And they'll say what Jews say
On Hanukah, Passover, and Purim:
They tried to kill us but failed,
So let's eat delicacies and tell funny stories
To keep living well,
Lest we sink to the bottom of memory's
Black hole of tears
And shame
And fury.

3.

Let's be like dreamers again. In days to come
When Israelis and Palestinians join their states,
We will look back at the children who learned
Both Arabic and Hebrew,
For in the supple and sinuous letters,
They saw the face of one land
That two peoples love.
May our peoples be blessed,
For renewing themselves
In a land of dreams

יְבוֹרְכוּ עַמֵּינוּ
שֶׁמִתְחַדְשִׁים
בְּאֶרֶץ חֲלוֹמוֹת.

Yevorchu ameinu
shemitchadshim
b'eretz chalomot.

Candle Lighting for Shavuot

Blessed is our wise tradition,
Inspiring us to light candles for this special day.
May our people and our world be blessed
With the light of hope and peace.

בְּרוּכָה אַתְּ, מְסוֹרְתֵנוּ הַנְּבוֹנָה
הַמְעוֹרֶרֶת אוֹתָנוּ לְהַדְלִיק נֵר שֶׁל יוֹם טוֹב.
יְבוֹרַךְ עַמֵנוּ וְעוֹלָמֵנוּ
בְּאוֹר הַתִּקְוָה וְהַשָּׁלוֹם.

Bruchah m'sorateinu hanvonah
ham'oreret otanu l'hadlik neir shel yom tov.
Y'vorach ameinu v'olameinu
b'or hatikvah v'hashalom.

Kiddush for Shavuot

Blessed are you, fertile world,
Forming the fruit of the vine.
Blessed is our wise tradition,
Passing down to us festivals for joy:
This holiday of Shavuot,
A time to lift up our first fruits,
A time to envision our destination,
And a time to make Jewish teachings new.
We lovingly welcome
This holiday of Shavuot.

Blessed are you, living world,
That has kept us alive, sustained us
And allowed us to reach this moment.

בְּרוּכָה אַתְּ, תֵּבֵל פּוֹרָה,
יוֹצֶרֶת פְּרִי הַגֶּפֶן.
בְּרוּכָה מְסוֹרָתֵנוּ הַנְּבוֹנָה
הַמַּנְחִילָה לָנוּ חַגִּים וּזְמַנִּים לְשָׂשׂוֹן:
אֶת חַג הַשָּׁבוּעוֹת הַזֶּה,
זְמַן לְהַעֲלוֹת אֶת בִּכּוּרֵנוּ,
זְמַן לַחֲזוֹת אֶת יַעֲדֵנוּ,
וּזְמַן לְחַדֵּשׁ אֶת תּוֹרָתֵנוּ.
אֶת חַג הַשָּׁבוּעוֹת הַזֶּה
בְּאַהֲבָה וּבְרָצוֹן נְקַבְּלָה.

בָּרוּךְ אַתָּה, עוֹלָם חַי,
שֶׁהֶחֱיָנוּ, וְקִיְּמָנוּ, וְהִגִּיעָנוּ לַזְּמַן הַזֶּה.

Bruchah at teiveil porah,
yotzeret p'ri hagafen.
Bruchah m'sorateinu hanvonah
hamanchilah lanu
chagim uz'manim l'sason:
et chag haShavuot hazeh,
z'man lahaalot et bikureinu,
z'man lachazot et yaadeinu,
uz'man l'chadeish et Torateinu.
Et chag haShavuot hazeh
B'ahavah uv'ratzon n'kablah

Baruch ata olam chai,
shehecheyanu v'kiy'manu
v'higi-anu laz'man hazeh.

For Shavuot: A New Old Religion

A new old religion
Without a commander
Or commandments engraved in stone:
At its center,
How Ruth followed Naomi out of love,
How Boaz opened his hand
And his heart to Naomi and Ruth,
How he gave them six overflowing
Measures of barley,
How he prevented his young men
From harassing the attractive stranger.
How he bought an unneeded field
To heal a broken Naomi.
The lion will not lie down with the lamb.
With kindness,
The world to come can come now.

Blessed is our tradition,
For speaking the Torah of kindness.

בְּרוּכָה מְסוֹרָתֵנוּ
שֶׁתּוֹרַת חֶסֶד עַל לְשׁוֹנָהּ.

Bruchah m'sorateinu
sheTorat chesed al l'shonah.

For Tisha b'Av: Birth Pangs

Jerusalem that was destroyed is rebuilt,
A city of two peoples, if not more.
We say, "renew our days as of old,"
Though we know we can't.
We mark a few days in our calendar
So as not to forget,
But what woman would give birth
A second time
If not for forgetting
The pangs of the first?

May our people be blessed
In giving birth to new days.

יְבוֹרַךְ עַמֵּנוּ
שֶׁמּוֹלִיד יָמִים חֲדָשִׁים.

Y'vorach ameinu
shemolid yomim chadashim.

Blessings for Various Occasions

Blessings for Food and Drink

Blessings Before a Meal

Blessed are you, generous Earth,
For providing us with food.

בְּרוּכָה אַתּ, תֵּבֵל נְדִיבָה, שֶׁמְסַפֶּקֶת לָנוּ אוֹכֶל.

*Bruchah at, teiveil n'divah,
shem'sapeket lanu ochel.*

(*When the meal includes bread*)
Blessed is the way
Bread is brought forth from the earth.

בָּרוּךְ הַתַּהֲלִיךְ שֶׁמוֹצִיא לֶחֶם מִן הָאָרֶץ.

*Baruch hatahalich
shemotzi lechem min haaretz.*

Blessing for Drinking Water

Blessed are you, overflowing Earth,
Giving us water to drink.

בְּרוּכָה אַתּ, תֵּבֵל שׁוֹפַעַת, הַנוֹתֶנֶת לָנוּ מַיִם לִשְׁתּוֹת.

*Bruchah at, teiveil shofaat,
hanotenet lanu mayim lishtot.*

Blessing over Wine or Grape Juice

Blessed are you, fertile Earth,
Forming the fruit of the vine.

בְּרוּכָה אַתְּ, תֵּבֵל פּוֹרָה, יוֹצֶרֶת פְּרִי הַגֶּפֶן.

*Bruchah at, teiveil porah,
yotzeret p'ri hagafen.*

Blessing over Fruits

Blessed are you, fertile Earth,
Forming the fruits of trees.

בְּרוּכָה אַתְּ, תֵּבֵל פּוֹרָה, יוֹצֶרֶת פְּרִי הָעֵץ.

*Bruchah at, teiveil porah,
yotzeret p'ri ha'eitz.*

Blessing over Vegetables

Blessed are you, fertile Earth,
Forming the produce of fields.

בְּרוּכָה אַתְּ, תֵּבֵל פּוֹרָה, יוֹצֶרֶת פְּרִי הַשָּׂדֶה.

Bruchah at, teiveil porah,
yotzeret p'ri hasadeh.

Blessing After a Meal

May what we ate satisfy us,
May what we drank be for our health,
May what we left over be a blessing,
Providing for those who thirst and hunger.
Blessed are you, Earth, our mother,
Nourishing all that lives.

מַה שֶׁאָכַלְנוּ יִהְיֶה לַשׂוֹבַע,
וּמַה שֶׁשָּׁתִינוּ יִהְיֶה לִרְפוּאָה,
וּמַה שֶׁהוֹתַרְנוּ יִהְיֶה לִבְרָכָה,
לְסַפֵּק לַצְּמֵאִים וְלָרְעֵבִים.
בְּרוּכָה אַתְּ, תֵּבֵל אִמֵּנוּ, הַזָּנָה אֶת הַכֹּל.

Mah she-achalnu yih'yeh lasova,
uma sheshatinu yih'yeh lirfuah,
uma shehotarnu yih'yeh liv'rachah,
l'sapeik latz'mei-im v'lar'eivim.
Bruchah at, teiveil imeinu,
hazanah et hakol.

Blessings for Sight and Smell

Blessing on Seeing a Rainbow

Blessed are you, astonishing universe,
Which alone makes wonders.

בָּרוּךְ אַתָּה, יְקוּם מַדְהִים, עוֹשֶׂה נִפְלָאוֹת לְבַדּוֹ.

*Baruch ata, y'kum madhim,
oseih nifla-ot l'vado.*

Blessing on Seeing the Ocean

Blessed are you, magnetic world,
Drawing the sea toward the land.

בָּרוּךְ אַתָּה, עוֹלָם מַגְנֵטִי, הַמוֹשֵׁךְ אֶת הַיָּם לְאַדְמוֹת תֵּבֵל.

*Baruch ata, olam magneti,
hamosheich et hayam l'admot teiveil.*

Blessing on Seeing Mountains

Blessed are you, evolving world, forming mountains.

בְּרוּכָה אַתְּ, תֵּבֵל מִתְפַּתַּחַת, יוֹצֶרֶת הָרִים.

Bruchah at, teiveil mitpatachat, yotseret harim.

Blessing on Smelling Fragrant Flowers

Blessed are you, procreative Earth,
Attracting species one to another.

בְּרוּכָה אַתְּ, תֵּבֵל רָבָה,
שְׁמוֹשֶׁכֶת אֶת הַבְּרִיוֹת אַחַת לְאַחוֹתָה.

*Bruchah at, teiveil ravah,
shemoshechet et habri-ot achat l'achota.*

Blessing for Reaching a Milestone

For an individual:
Blessed are you, living world,
Which has kept me alive, sustained me
And allowed me to reach this moment.

בָּרוּךְ אַתָּה, עוֹלָם חַי,
שֶׁהֶחֱיָנִי, וְקִיְּמָנִי, וְהִגִּיעָנִי לַזְּמַן הַזֶּה.

Baruch ata, olam chai,
shehecheyani, v'kiy'mani,
v'higi-ani laz'man hazeh.

For a group:
Blessed are you, living world,
That has kept us alive, sustained us
And allowed us to reach this moment.

בָּרוּךְ אַתָּה, עוֹלָם חַי,
שֶׁהֶחֱיָנוּ, וְקִיְּמָנוּ, וְהִגִּיעָנוּ לַזְּמַן הַזֶּה.

Baruch ata, olam chai,
shehecheyanu v'kiy'manu
v'higi-anu laz'man hazeh.

Blessing for a Transition

Blessed are you, world of changes.

בְּרוּכָה אַתְּ, תֵּבַל שֶׁל שִׁינוּיִם.

Bruchah at, teiveil shel shinuyim.

Wedding Blessings

Blessings of the Officiant

Blessed be all
Who are here to witness
This covenant of lovers.
Blessed be this community and its love.
You are welcome here.

The Giving of Rings

I am my beloved's and my beloved is mine.
Take me as a seal on your heart,
A brace for your arm,
For love is as fierce as death.

אֲנִי לְדוֹדִי וְדוֹדִי לִי.
שִׂימֵנִי כַחוֹתָם עַל לִבֶּךָ, כַּחוֹתָם עַל זְרוֹעֶךָ.
כִּי עַזָּה כַמָּוֶת אַהֲבָה.

Ani l'dodi v'dodi li.
Simeini kachotam al libecha,
kachotam al z'ro-echa.
Ki azah kamavet ahavah.
(Song of Songs 6:3, 8:6)

The Seven Blessings of the Congregation

1.

Blessed are you, fertile Earth,
Forming the fruit of the vine.

2.

Blessed are you, fertile Earth,
Seeding and growing all that lives.

3.

Blessed are you, fertile Earth,
Allowing human beings to evolve.

4.

Blessed are you, fertile Earth,
Creating coupling.

5.

Sing exaltedly, you who know of barrenness,
At the coupling of these your children.
Blessed is our joyous tradition,
Making the Jewish people glad
To welcome them.

6.

Rejoice, rejoice, beloved friends,
As you thrilled at your first embrace.
Blessed are you, fertile Earth,
Who makes glad the bride and groom,
The groom and groom, the bride and bride.

7.

Blessed are you, fertile Earth,
Creating brides and grooms, happiness and joy,
Gladness and gaiety, song and ululation,
Love and companionship, peace and friendship.
May we speedily hear
The voices of brides and grooms
Coming from their wedding canopies,
And those of young people from their parties of song.
Blessed are you, fertile Earth,
Allowing the bride and groom,
the groom and groom, the bride and bride,
Each to rejoice with the other.

Blessing for Healing

We bless you—
Doctors, nurses, and therapists,
That your hearts be tender
And your judgment level-headed.

נְבָרֵךְ אֶתְכֶם—
רוֹפְאִים, אַחָיוֹת, וּמְטַפְּלִים—
שֶׁלְּבָבוֹתֵיכֶם תִּהְיוּ רַכִּים
וְדַעְתְּכֶם שְׁקוּלָה.

N'vareich etchem—
rofim, achayot, um'taplim—
shel'vavoteichem tih'yu rakim
v'daatchem sh'kulah.

To those who are suffering—
We wish you complete healing
Of body and of soul
And we bless you with patience, hope,
And the strength to be healed.

נְבָרֵךְ אֶתְכֶם שֶׁכּוֹאֲבִים רְפוּאָה שְׁלֵמָה—
רְפוּאַת הַנֶּפֶשׁ וּרְפוּאַת הַגּוּף—
וּנְאַחֵל לָכֶם סַבְלָנוּת, תִּקְוָה, וְכוֹחַ לְהֵרָפֵא.

N'vareich etchem sheko-avim r'fuah shleimah—
r'fuat hanefesh ur'fuat haguf—
un'acheil lachem savlanut, tikvah, v'ko-ach l'heirafei.

Declaration on Hearing of a Death

Such is the destiny of all that live.

זֶה הַגּוֹרָל לְכָל חַי.

Zeh hagoral l'chol chai.

Walking the Mourner's Path

At the Graveside

We give our dead to the earth
From which they came,
Permitting the earth to embrace
The one we loved,
Fulfilling what our father Abraham said:
"I am but dust and ashes."
Without our consent we are born,
Against our will we die.
We too, standing here today
By the open grave,
Will enter it one day
At an unexpected hour.
All the doors of our hearts are open
To the pain of our loss.
Let us begin to free the memory
Of the one we loved
From our pain,
Being grateful for the good
In the life that was lived.

Response to the Mourners:

May you be comforted.
תְּנוּחָמוּ.
T'nuchamu.

For Those We Loved

As we say *yitgadal v'yitkadash*,
We make holy whatever we loved about you
When you were alive.
As we say *yitgadal v'yitkadash*,
We grow the kindnesses
That you did.
As we say *yitgadal v'yitkadash*,
We bind your soul in the bonds of life,
Remembering you each day.

בְּאָמְרֵנוּ יִתְגַּדַּל וְיִתְקַדָּשׁ,
אֲנַחְנוּ מַקְדִּישִׁים אֶת כָּל מַה שֶׁאָהַבְנוּ בָּכֶם
בְּחַיֵּיכֶם.
בְּאָמְרֵנוּ יִתְגַּדַּל וְיִתְקַדָּשׁ,
אֲנַחְנוּ מַכְפִּילִים אֶת הַחֲסָדִים
שֶׁגְּמַלְתֶּם.
בְּאָמְרֵנוּ יִתְגַּדַּל וְיִתְקַדָּשׁ,
אֲנַחְנוּ קוֹשְׁרִים אֶת נִשְׁמוֹתֵיכֶם בִּצְרוֹר הַחַיִּים
בְּזָכְרֵנוּ אֶתְכֶם יוֹם־יוֹם.

B'omreinu yitgadal v'yitkadash,
anachnu makdishim et kol mah
she-ahavnu bachem b'chayeichem.
B'omreinu yitgadal v'yitkadash,
anachnu koshrim et nishmoteichem
b'tzror hachayim
b'zochreinu etchem yom yom.

For a Person who Died without Family

Our love for them and their love for us—
Links on a unique chain.

For Alienated Relationships

I can't say kaddish for this person who died.
The connection between us is broken
Beyond repair.
Shall I still carry this heavy burden?
If I lay it down,
Can I again know peace?

At a House of Mourning

Remembering a Good-Hearted Man

Fortunate is the man
Who lived to love his family.
Fortunate is the partner
Who lived with him in mutual love.
Fortunate are his children,
Whom he loved unconditionally.
Fortunate are the grandchildren
Who entwined around him in love.
Fortunate are the great grandchildren,
Who will be told the story of his life.
Fortunate is the community who befriended a man
Who loved and was loved by so many.
The descendants of a good-hearted man
Are respected in our land.
His legacy endures.

Remembering a Good-Hearted Woman

Fortunate is the woman
Who lived to love her family.
Fortunate is the partner
Who lived with her in mutual love.
Fortunate are her sons and daughters,
Whom she loved unconditionally.
Fortunate are the grandchildren
Who entwined around her in love.
Fortunate are the great grandchildren,
Who will be told the story of her life.
Fortunate is the community
Who befriended a woman
Who loved and was loved by so many.
The descendants of a good-hearted woman
Are respected in our land.
Her legacy endures.

A New Kaddish

The sea splits, the heavens open,
A man dead for three days walks the highway,
Horse and rider fly to the holy city,
The fat man comes down the chimney—
O civilized world,
Drowning in a sea of unreality.

Let's form the next version:
Make the world holy
Without the old stories and masks,
Paint with all the hues,
Play with all the instruments,
Write with each alphabet
Names of all the creatures,
A great name that includes them all,
Serving us as both lament and prayer:
Yitgadal v'yitkadash shmay rabba
Let us make that name great and holy.

Musical Notation: Thirteen Songs

The music presented in this section is available for use in any congregation. If reproduced for communal singing, it should be copied as printed here. If used in any performance for which admission is charged, royalties apply as indicated.

The thirteen songs are set to eight different texts, presented below in the order in which they appear in this Siddur. Where there are multiple versions of a single text, they are presented alphabetically by last name of the music's composer.

A Blessing for the Light and the Dark

Herbert J. Levine, lyrics
Rabbi Shefa Gold, music

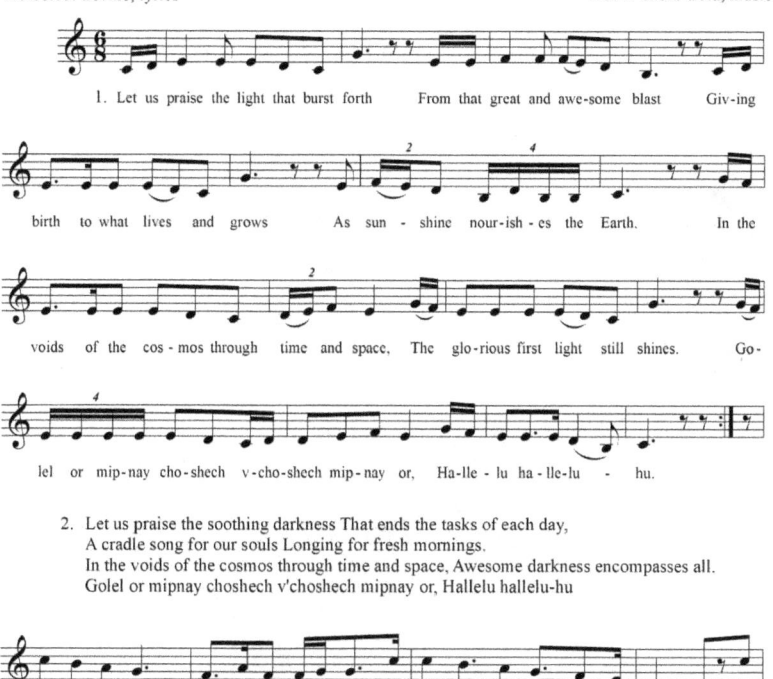

2. Let us praise the soothing darkness That ends the tasks of each day,
   A cradle song for our souls Longing for fresh mornings.
   In the voids of the cosmos through time and space, Awesome darkness encompasses all.
   Golel or mipnay choshech v'choshech mipnay or, Hallelu hallelu-hu

© 2023 Herbert J. Levine (ASCAP) and Shefa Gold
All rights reserved

A Blessing for the Light and the Dark

Blessing for the Light and the Dark

you, in-fi-nite u-ni-verse, Re-veal-ing the light and the dark. Re-veal-ing the light and the dark.

2. Let us praise the soothing darkness
That ends the tasks of each day,
A cradle song for our souls
Longing for fresh mornings.

In the voids of the cosmos through time and space,
Awesome darkness encompasses all.
In the voids of the cosmos through time and space,
Awesome darkness encompasses all.

Blessed are you, infinite universe,
Blessed are you, infinite universe,
Blessed are you, infinite universe,
Revealing the light and the dark.
Revealing the light and the dark.

A Blessing for the Light and the Dark

2. Let us praise the soothing darkness
That ends the tasks of each day,
A cradle song for our souls
Longing for fresh mornings.
In the voids of the cosmos through time and space,
Awesome darkness encompasses all.

© 2023 Herbert J. Levine (ASCAP) and Zach Mayer (SESAC)
All rights reserved

A Blessing for Love

Herbert J. Levine, lyrics
Rabbi Shefa Gold, music

2. We are the love that shines through the darkness, Descended from those who came down from the trees,
   We are the love that shines through the darkness, Descended from those who came down from the trees,
   Imbued with knowing right from wrong: So with justice, let's pursue what is right.

3. We are the love that shines through the darkness, A radiance so bright it lights up the world,
   We are the love that shines through the darkness, A radiance so bright it lights up the world,
   Carrying the love of generations: With strength, let's chant songs of love.

© 2023 Herbert J. Levine (ASCAP) and Shefa Gold
All rights reserved

A Blessing for Love

2. We are the love that shines through the darkness,
   Descended from those who came down from trees,
   Imbued with knowing right from wrong:
   With justice, let's pursue what is right.

   Blessed are you, O shining world,
   Blessed are you, O shining world,
   Blessed are you, O shining world,
   Reveling in love, Reveling in love.

3. We are the love that shines through darkness,
   A radiance so bright it lights up the world,
   Carrying the love of generations:
   With strength, let's chant these songs of love.

   Blessed are you, O shining world,
   Blessed are you, O shining world,
   Blessed are you, O shining world,
   Reveling in love, Reveling in love.

© 2023 Herbert J. Levine (ASCAP) and Eileen Kozloff (BMI)
All rights reserved

A Blessing for Love

Herbert J. Levine, lyrics
Zach Mayer, music

2. We are the love that shines through darkness,
   Descended from those who came down from trees,
   Imbued with knowing right from wrong,
   Imbued with knowing right from wrong:
   So with justice, let's pursue what is right.

3. We are the love that shines through darkness,
   A radiance so bright it lights up the world,
   Carrying the love of generations,
   Carrying the love of generations:
   With strength, let's chant songs of love.

© 2023 Herbert J. Levine (ASCAP) and Zach Mayer (SESAC)
All rights reserved

A Blessing for Redemption

© 2023 Herbert J. Levine (ASCAP) and Zach Mayer (SESAC)
All rights reserved

A Blessing for Holiness

© 2023 Herbert J. Levine (ASCAP) and Shefa Gold
All rights reserved

A Blessing for Gratitude

2. It takes a lifetime to learn how to live,
   To sort through the stuff that fills up our days,
   To weigh and to measure just what to claim
   To know that enough, know that enough,
   know that enough is as good as a feast?

3. Let's sit at nightfall with those that we love
   And light a candle to greet the dark,
   Clasp our hands as we bless the bread
   And know that enough, know that enough,
   know that enough is as good as a feast?

4. Let's open our hearts to the joy and the pain,
   The bitter and sweet of the knowledge we've gained
   And Sweetly surrender to what we can't change
   To know that enough, know that enough,
   know that enough is as good as a feast?

© 2023 Herbert J. Levine (ASCAP) and Eileen Kozloff (BMI)
All rights reserved

A Blessing for Peace

© 2023 Herbert J. Levine (ASCAP) and Shefa Gold
All rights reserved

Welcoming Shabbat

© 2023 Herbert J. Levine (ASCAP) and Eileen Kozloff (BMI)
All rights reserved

Welcoming Shabbat

Herbert J. Levine, lyrics　　　　　　　　　　　Zach Mayer, music

© 2023 Herbert J. Levine (ASCAP) and Zach Mayer (SESAC)
All rights reserved

For Those We Loved

© 2023 Herbert J. Levine (ASCAP) and Shefa Gold
All rights reserved

Afterword

Blessed Are You, Wondrous Universe: A Siddur for Seekers might well have been called "Siddur for a New Paradigm." The term paradigm entered general usage with Thomas Kuhn's book, *The Structure of Scientific Revolutions* (1962). Rather than seeing science as the steady accumulation of evidence resulting in the continuous diffusion of knowledge, Kuhn introduced the idea that scientific models of reality emerge as revolutionary shifts in how we think about the world. Such ruptures result in new paradigms for how we seek out and interpret evidence. He further showed how such shifts characterize intellectual trends that extend beyond the confines of science. Copernicus's conclusions based on his observations of the heavens, confirmed by Galileo's careful measurements, caused a rupture in the geocentric cosmology of Christianity. The work of Lyell in geology and Darwin in biology, uncovering the immense age of the earth and the evolutionary adaptation and emergence of new species, changed how we view the history of all life on this planet, in effect, overturning the Bible as a source of authoritative truth. Einstein, in his turn, gave us a new basis for understanding the universe as a continuum of energy in space and time stretching back to the Big Bang.

Because of the paradigm shift initiated by Einstein's insights, we have come to understand that human energy and matter are continuous with what we see above us in the stars. When American philosopher and psychologist, William James, coined the term "multiverse" to refer to the vastly different worldviews held by people in the same society, he could not have foreseen that his term would one day be paired with quantum physics to become the basis of a new cosmological paradigm, which posits many universes existing simultaneously. Physics continues to come up with new thought experiments, such as string theory and dimensions beyond those of time and space, which have some of us thinking about living in a multiverse with competing realities, whether through science fiction or postmodernist claims for the impossibility of finding truth. These are paradigms in the making, still seeking a foothold.

Each scientific paradigm shift produces analogous developments in the social sciences and humanities, though sometimes the shift begins in humanistic disciplines. One such decisive shift in the humanities came in the late 19th century with Emil Durkheim's historicist sociology of religion. He helped us step back from our religious practices and understand that a monarchical society, for instance, would inevitably frame its idea of God in monarchical terms. Such a religion would naturally include an earthly temple that would serve as the god-king's palace, where his priests could be fed and the sovereign god could be propitiated with sacrificial offerings. As Judaism evolved to accommodate a post-Temple reality, Jewish liturgy maintained the metaphors of this monarchic paradigm, which has brought us to the impasse in which many of us contemporary Jews now find ourselves: with an outmoded liturgy that does not speak to the reality of our experience.

An American contemporary of Durkheim, John Dewey, also advocated for a sociological approach to religion, leading him to a new search for meaning. In *A Common Faith* (1934), Dewey argued that religion needed to be reconstructed along naturalistic and democratic lines befitting life in a pragmatic American society. Mordecai Kaplan, arguably the most influential American rabbi of the twentieth century, applied these Deweyan ideas to his own reconstruction of Judaism, famously seeing Judaism as an evolving religious civilization, rather than a religion rooted in dogma. It was quite natural in the American context to eliminate the ancient Israelite concept of being a chosen people because that belief could not easily coexist with democratic norms.

Closer to our own time, in the 1980s, Zalman Schachter-Shalomi advocated for renewing Judaism by applying to it James Lovelock's Gaian hypothesis. Lovelock proposed that Earth had evolved into one, giant living organism, of which we humans are the most highly conscious antennae, certainly the most verbal, who can gather the information necessary to steer its course. Recent scholarship on the vast communication networks that exist underground among trees and fungi has added significantly to the idea that we live in a planetary ecosystem with many sensing parts contributing to the welfare of the whole. In Schachter-Shalomi's paradigm-shift theology, God is almost wholly identified with this immanent dimension as Gaia, with a greatly diminished role for any notion of divine transcendence, but with an increased role for humans in shaping Earth's destiny.

In an essay published in *Tikkun* in 2015, Shaul Magid called for new Jewish liturgy that would be responsive to Schachter-Shalomi's paradigm-shift theology. In a sidebar piece written shortly before he died, Schachter-Shalomi noted that the time for such new liturgies was indeed coming. Any words repeated by rote can eventually become hollow. So new liturgy needs to be rooted in language that passes our tests for what is true of the universe and yet be aspirational and emotive enough to resonate with our hearts. This siddur seeks to distill the essence of the traditional Jewish service by following its order and forms of blessing, while making the universe the subject of our wonder, and the earth, its creatures, and the universal values within the Jewish tradition the subjects of our devotion.

This Siddur's Values and Practices

I believe that the practices that *Siddur for Seekers* offers—consecrating the cosmos through blessings, affirming that the world we live in is sacred, holding up for praise the most universal values in the Jewish tradition—will be good for Jews and good for our world. It can be justly said that universalism as an ideal began from the premise that the God of Israel spoke to and for the whole world. The prophets of Israel were the first to realize that the justice and mercy that they advocated were not limited to a single people. The Israelites were the first people to perceive the universe as a single whole. But they were also a particular people, with a language and history of their own. *Siddur for Seekers* blends the particularism of a reborn Jewish language, Hebrew, and the liturgical framework of a particular people, the Jews, with the universal aspirations of humanity for living in a just, peaceful, and sustainable world.

Monotheism has been a useful tool, helping humanity step beyond the constant warfare between opposing forces represented in polytheist mythology. It has simplified the quest for explaining the origins and governance of the world, but it did so by incorporating the origin of evil within the godhead, which created an unresolvable conundrum for believers in a good God. A flawed monotheism cannot be the final step in the evolution of planetary or cosmic consciousness. Four centuries ago, Spinoza asserted that God was the universe, saying in effect that all that exists is divine. This siddur makes a materialist counterclaim: that all that is, simply is. The world is the world, so what we see is what we get. What we can know by the laws of science and our powers of cognition is the only revelation we can access.

The language of this siddur is rooted in a commitment to a

Jewish idiom that accords with both science and wonder. *O-lam* is a good choice to name our universe, because the ancient Hebrew word connotes both time and space. The biblical word for existence, *yi-koom*, from the Hebrew word to build or establish, is also a good choice, because it connotes the process that led to the universe we now inhabit. Another ancient name, *tay-vayl*, denotes our earthly habitation. In biblical Hebrew, all three terms overlap. In these prayerful poems, I deliberately address *o-lam*, *tay-vayl*, and *yi-koom* without any intervening definite article. Adding the definite article *'ha'* would have focused us on the thingness of 'the world' and landed us in the conundrum of separating ourselves from the world. But when we address them directly, my hope is that we learn to make them living presences within us, rather than dead entities outside us.

On Praising and Blessing in a New Key

As readers encounter the formulations, "Blessed are you, wondrous universe," or "Blessed are you, fruitful world," a few questions tend to arise. What do I mean by the notion of blessing? Why have I personified the universe and our earthly world as entities that can be addressed, even if they cannot speak back? What does it mean to call the universe sacred, when Jews have always used the word *ka-dosh* to refer to times, places, people, and actions set apart by God? By addressing the universe as a 'you,' are we still including ourselves within it?

Human beings bless one another all the time with wishes for good health and success. "Go in peace and return in peace," we say, or "A blessing on your head," using traditional ritual language without invoking a divine source for our hopes. By using such words, we make ourselves agents and channels of good will to the person we address. We gain access to a dimension of life that expresses our hopes and aspirations so that our lives can partake of deeper meaning and purpose. In conveying such blessings, we are performing actions using the performative dimension of language, much as we would if we were to say at a certain time and place and with a ring placed on our finger, "I do." By saying, "Blessed are you, abundant world," or "O blessed, infinite universe," we shift our consciousness to the blessings that flow from one part of nature to us, another part of nature. To my ears, by turning to the universe as a 'you,' we make ourselves humble in the face of the awesome unfolding that stretches from the Big Bang to ourselves. We perceive and act as separate selves, yet we are as much part of the universe that we're blessing as anything else in it. Moreover, we are the only creatures in the universe that can call it blessed and wondrous.

Just as we establish a channel for blessing with our words, so we are responsible for the creation of holiness and sacredness. Holiness is not something that inheres in things. It is a quality that we attribute to things and to actions. Through our ritual language and actions, we set them apart and elevate them. We sanctify them. If we do not sanctify the Sabbath, for instance, then we experience it as just another Friday night or Saturday. For those of us who make this prayer book our own, this siddur's uses of the words "holy" and "sacred" should gradually transform our attitudes to what surrounds and includes us.

Moving from the notion of blessing and sanctifying to praying, I find it helpful to think of praying with the universe, with the earth, as a dialogue with oneself. The poetic praises and blessings in this siddur are meant to align those who use its language with the values the words evoke. Such value-laden speech acts hold me to account. I build on the insights of the great American Pragmatist philosopher, William James, who said that we hold on to beliefs because we find those beliefs useful to how we want to live our lives.

The core principles of traditional Jewish belief can be summed up under three basic rubrics: that 'God' is a Creator, a Revealer, and a Redeemer. This propositional version of Judaism is increasingly unconvincing, so more and more people with Jewish identities describe themselves as Jews with no religion. Those who accept the scientific worldview cannot believe that our world was created, because we know that it evolved and is still evolving. Jews who have studied religion, sociology, or literature understand that the Torah was not dictated by a supernatural being, but that it came together over centuries at the hands of human authors, who claimed divine authority to lead their fellow Jews toward what they conceived as good ends. Jews who have studied history understand the negative impact of messianic figures on the Jewish people, so they do not look forward to a time when the human future will be shaped by a 'Messiah' with 'divine' powers. Instead, they rely on themselves and their fellow human beings to shape our future world. In short, for contemporary Jews with a modern, secular worldview, there is no Creation, no Revelation, no Redemption. So why do Jews in the liberal branches of Judaism continue to evoke in their worship the God Who Creates, Reveals, and Redeems?

    The answer is that rituals engage not just our minds, but our bodies and our emotions as well. The traditional language and melodies of religious services are replete with positive emotional resonances that give many people a sense of security and well-being. Given the magnetic, emotive power of traditional rituals, I have been asked how I can expect people to adopt new liturgical language. To be sure, by accepting new language for prayer, there is going to be a feeling of losing familiar connections to our ancestors who said these same words. But given that the language of the traditional siddur has become increasingly hollow for so many of those reciting it, how long can nostalgia alone justify our using words that we know are not true for us? I believe that if we combine new words with uplifting melodies, we will get both intellectual excitement and emotional soothing, so that new prayers may have a chance of taking root in our hearts and minds.

In the past, our people's dialogue has been with a personified supernatural being, but this involves us in dallying dangerously with unreality and constituting religion as a form of shared delusion, with all the negative effects this has on our larger culture:

> The sea splits, the heavens open,
> A man dead for three days walks the highway,
> Horse and rider fly to the holy city,
> The fat man comes down the chimney—
> O civilized world, drowning in a sea of unreality.
>
> Let's form the next version:
> Make the world holy
> Without the old stories and masks…

To form that next version, let's be in a reverential dialogue with the vast universe and the world around us. Seeing the world as merely secular is surely one of the factors that has led humanity to abuse our planetary home. So it's time to try out an alternative—seeing the world as sacred. If we can learn to sanctify our world, perhaps we can still save it from our own worst impulses and preserve it for our descendants and all the creatures that dwell with us on this planet.

Acknowledgments

Even a siddur written by an individual emerges from within a community. I would like to acknowledge my profound debt to the community that motivated and encouraged me. The list is roughly chronological, dating back to 2015. I want to thank:

Rabbi Shaul Magid, for calling for new liturgy to express the paradigm change from supernaturalist to cosmos-centered worship implied by Schachter-Shalomi's theology.

The late Rabbi Michael Lerner, editor of *Tikkun*, and Lawrence Bush, editor of *Jewish Currents*, for finding a place for my poems and prose that led to this work.

Nina Wacholder, for offering the generative insight that my poems rooted in science "pass the truth test."

Rabbi Linda Motzkin, for her beautiful visual portrayal of my liturgical phrase, *barukh ata olam*.

Ruth Goldston, for being a great cheerleader: for suggesting the possibility of setting my poetry to music when she first heard it, for creating a musical setting for my poem "A Song for Gratitude," for asking me to compose a psalm for her father's funeral, which became part of the Siddur, and for hearing it all as prayer.

Larry Yudelson, publisher of Ben Yehuda Press, for including my two books of bi-lingual poems, *Words for Blessing the World* and *An Added Soul: Poems for a New Old Religion* in Ben Yehuda's Jewish Poetry Series.

Editors of the journal, *Slant,* for publishing "The Woman Who Loves Wetlands," presented here in a shorter form as "A Blessing for Species: Birds."

The late Ross London, for responding in *Tikkun* magazine to my books as calls for a "third way in Judaism," neither religious, nor secular, but growing out of both realms.

Rabbi Aubrey Glazer, for hearing in my poems Spinoza's prayer, as he explained in the pages of *Tikkun*.

Rabbis Adam Chalom, Fred Dobbs, Rachel Hersh, and Suri Kriger, for making my poems part of their congregations' liturgies and discourse, which gave me a push toward composing this siddur.

Rabbi Haviva Ner David for responding so powerfully to my "Song for Gratitude" in her memoir, *Dreaming Against the Current: A Rabbi's Soul Journey.*

The late Adina Newberg, whose suggestions for the Hebrew of my second volume of poetry have carried over to this one.

Hanoch Guy and Rabbi Tzemah Yoreh, for their generosity in reviewing the Hebrew of my poems and blessings and suggesting differing alternatives, and Rabbi Miriam Margles, for being a sounding board for testing the Hebrew of my holiday blessings.

Aliza Arzt, for assuring that the nikkud (the points under the Hebrew letters) passes muster.

Rabbi Goldie Milgram, Rabbi Tzemah Yoreh, Rabbi Jeffrey

Schein, and SAJ congregant, Ellen Gesmer, for giving me venues for discussing this project with congregants and colleagues.

The late Rabbi Everett Gendler, for expressing the hope that this work could help heal the rift between secular and religious Jews and their opposing worldviews.

Grace Flisser, Stephen Jones, Michael Metelits, and Ruth Spack, for helpful comments on my explanatory prose.

Yosaif August, for urging me to claim a bold title for this book.

Simcha Raphael for being in dialogue with me on so many levels, for identifying the book's subtitle in my prose, and for suggesting that I write a Kaddish for someone from whom we are estranged.

Ori Alon, for helping me to work through what such a Kaddish might say.

Rabbi Marcia Prager, for formulating in the language of a *d'var torah* the kernel of the Tu B'Shvat poem in this volume.

Rabbi Geoff Basik for requesting a suite of poems for Havdalah.

Janice Halpern, for requesting a piece modeled on Hashkivenu, "Cause us to lie down in peace," here called "Prayer Before Bedtime."

Joseph Rosenstein for his suggestion that there could be a separate blessing for drinking water.

Russell Berman, Ralph Halpern, and Norman Shore for conversations that helped me to place this endeavor in terms of my own history.

The late David Barcan, for creating "Songs for Blessing the World," made up of five musical settings for the Hebrew of my poems, and Joshua Ehrlich for orchestrating them in four-part harmony, listed individually at: http://www.joshehrlichmusic.com/arrangements

Juliet Spitzer, for composing a melody for an early draft of "A Blessing for Love."

Sharon Strassfeld and Rabbi William Cutter for finding a home for my lyric, "Let's be dreamers again" in the "Peace" movement of "The Abrahamic Symphony," available at https://www.youtube.com/watch?v=8CIslh04VVA.

Joey Weisenberg, the late Cantor Jack Kessler, Cantor Jonathan Friedmann, Rabbis Goldie Milgrom and Gila Rayzel Raphael, for helping me to look for composers to set my words to music.

Rabbi Shefa Gold, Eileen Kozloff, and Zach Mayer, my musical collaborators in creating thirteen melodies, for turning my poems on the page into living prayers, and James Cooper, for notating their music. The broader scope of their work is represented on their respective websites:

https://www.rabbishefagold.com/
http://www.eileenkozloff.com/
https://www.zachmayermusic.com/
https://modez.com/

Rabbi Shefa Gold, for permission to use her interpretive translation of Song of Songs 5:5.

Ellen Frankel, for graciously listening to and reading every word, in multiple versions, and giving her honest appraisal.

And all those who have tried out selections of this work with their havurot and congregations.

About the Author

Herbert Levine has previously written psalm-like bi-lingual poems, published in two volumes by Ben Yehuda Press: *Words for Blessing the World* (2017) and *An Added Soul: Poems for a New Old Religion* (2020). He is also a literary scholar with books to his credit on Yeats (*Yeats's Daimonic Renewal*, UMI Press, 1983) and on the Biblical Psalms (*Sing Unto God a New Song: A Contemporary Reading of the Psalms*, Indiana Univ. Press, 1995). He earned his BA at Harvard College and his Ph.D. at Princeton University.

His work in translation from the Hebrew, together with Reena M. Spicehandler, has appeared in two volumes in the Toby Press Agnon collection and their translations from Mendele Mocher Seforim, on Jewishfiction.net.

www.ingramcontent.com/pod-product-compliance
Lightning Source LLC
Chambersburg PA
CBHW050552160426
43199CB00015B/2635